ETHNIC TIMES

ETHNIC TIMES

Exploring Ethnonationalism in the Former Yugoslavia

Dusan Kecmanovic

Westport, Connecticut
London

Library of Congress Cataloging-in-Publication Data

Kecmanovic, Dusan.
    Ethnic times : exploring ethnonationalism in the former
  Yugoslavia / Dusan Kecmanovic.
      p. cm.
  Includes bibliographical references and index.
  ISBN 0–275–97461–8 (alk. paper)
    1. Yugoslavia—Ethnic relations. 2. Ethnicity—Yugoslavia.
  3. Nationalism—Yugoslavia. I. Title.
  DR1229.K43 2002
  305.8′009497—dc21   2001034627

British Library Cataloguing in Publication Data is available.

Library of Congress Catalog Card Number: 2001034627
ISBN: 0–275–97461–8

First published in 2002

Praeger Publishers, 88 Post Road West, Westport, CT 06881
An imprint of Greenwood Publishing Group, Inc.
www.praeger.com

Printed in the United States of America

The paper used in this book complies with the
Permanent Paper Standard issued by the National
Information Standards Organization (Z39.48–1984).

10 9 8 7 6 5 4 3 2 1

Contents

Introductory Remarks
1

Between Old and New Regimes
9

Why There Are so Many Faithful
17

**Journey Through Post-Yugoslavia States in the
Height of Ethnic Times**
21

Neither Sick nor Hale and Hearty
37

The Violence of Daily Life
45

The Agony and the Ecstasy of the Victim
53

His Father Saved Him
59

The Individual and the Collective in Ethnonationalism
67

A Good Enough Enemy
77

The Boomerang of Impassioned Bias
83

Endemic and Epidemic Ethnonationalists
87

Inverse Ethnonationalism
95

The Woes of Divided Loyalty
105

Ethnonationalism in the Genes
113

Brief Conversation with an Ethnonationalist about
Children from Ethnically Mixed Marriages
121

Is There Something Mentally Wrong with
Ethnonationalists?
123

Why Ethnonationalists Are Aggressive
129

Contents

vii

Ethnic Stereotypes in the Writings of Croatian
and Serbian Psychiatrists
137

Prove You're a Serb
157

Reactive Ethnonationalists
163

Obsession with Ethnicity
167

For Further Reading
173

Index
181

Introductory Remarks

In the last decade of the twentieth century, the area of what was once Yugoslavia experienced multiparty elections, changes in the regime, wars, and, above all, burgeoning ethnonationalistic views and passions. It was a time of great changes in the political, social, and economic life. Little remained as it had been in the mid-1980s. Privatization began and there was a rise in unemployment and general social uncertainty; in some places this was rapid, in others more gradual. In just a few years a small number of people became fantastically wealthy, while most were reduced to impoverishment. A large number of people, primarily younger and highly educated, left the country. Habits changed overnight, along with the names of streets, squares, and institutions. New school curricula were hastily written. Historical individuals regarded for decades as heroes and liberators became terrorists and occupiers. It was said that they had actually been terrorists and conquerors all along, but the previous regime had presented them incorrectly. Our best-loved writers, who had made us proud before the world, were black-listed; the busts of some of them were even toppled. People completely unknown to the broader public the week before became official interpreters of what was good for the nation and what was harmful to national interests. The uneducated, the frustrated, and the marginalized saw the new times as their chance of a lifetime, and perhaps their historical chance as well.

Longstanding friendships and marriages disintegrated simply because the friends and spouses were not of the same ethnic origin. Violence became the order of the day. National myths were resurrected on all sides. Great effort was put into concocting differences between the cultures of the ethnonational groups, and differences that actually did exist were enormously inflated. Brotherhood by faith became the strongest tie. The inhabitants of far-off countries and continents were recognized as brothers. Members of another religion who lived in the same neighborhood, worked at the same job, lived on the same street or in the same village became sworn enemies, or were simply unwelcome as people who could not and must not be trusted. In some environments, religious circles began to play an important role in governing state affairs.

For most people, the unexpected, overall transformation could not have been more profound. This book deals with different aspects of that transformation.

The chapter "Between Old and New Regimes" presents a typology of people's behavior during the transition period when the old regime had not disappeared entirely and the new regime had yet to take power.

One phenomenon was rather characteristic of the transition period: a great many people (re)turned to religion. The chapter "Why There Are so Many Faithful" tries to interpret the meaning of this phenomenon and determine how many of these new believers were real, genuine believers, and how many turned to religion because of the close link between faith and ethnicity.

Ethnonationalistic views and beliefs in the area of what was Yugoslavia were most apparent just before the disintegration of the second Yugoslavia and during the war (1991–95). Ethnonationalistic sentiments still run high over there. The author of this book traveled through part of Bosnia-Herzegovina, Croatia, and Serbia in the summer of 1992, and the chapter entitled "Journey Through Post-Yugoslavia States in the Height of Ethnic Times" presents his experiences with the different forms in which ethnonationalistic views and feelings are expressed.

The new times, as already mentioned, brought changes in the behavior of a large number of people. The changes were so sudden and so great that many truly wondered what was happening to most of their neighbors, fellow citizens, and fellow countrymen. How was it possible for them to become, seemingly overnight, highly aggressive and hostile towards those who were not of the same ethnic origin, and to advocate ideas and programs that previously had appeared completely foreign to them? Some even said that people had become mentally deranged. That was the easiest and fastest explanation. Just how accurate this was is treated in "Neither Sick nor Hale and Hearty."

The transition period was accompanied by a wave of violence, but it was not just the proponents of ethnic cleansing who acted violently. People started to have less consideration for the rights and interests of others, becoming increasingly heedless in the burning desire to grab as much as they could for themselves and their near and dear. "The Violence of Daily Life" discusses whether people were showing their true faces as soon as the social norms that keep this type of behavior at bay slackened or even lost importance, or whether the transition itself generated the increase in violence.

In the civil war that spread over most of the second Yugoslavia, members of each belligerent side looked upon themselves as victims and presented themselves as such to the international community. Why? Because the role of the victim, as paradoxical as it might sound, affords considerable privileges for those who succeed in convincing the world that although they might not be the only victims, they are certainly the greatest victims. The chapter "The Agony and the Ecstasy of the Victim" presents the attractive side of the role of victim and indicates the potential danger of insisting on this role, which always entails a high degree of innocence or lack of responsibility for the conflict in question. The victim counts on the right to start a new conflict in which he will "settle old accounts."

Ethnic times are times of turmoil in which some people lose and others find their (personal, familial, ethnonational) identity, in which many split up and some reunite with their close ones. The chapter "His Father Saved Him" describes the case of a man who reconciles with his long-resented father because of ethnic times.

The chapter "The Individual and the Collective in Ethnonationalism" tries to find an answer to the often raised question of whether certain people are more inclined towards ethnonationalism—in other words, whether some personality types have a special affinity for ethnonationalistic views and beliefs.

"A Good Enough Enemy" deals with the narcissism of small differences. The bloodiest civil wars are fought because the enemies have a lot in common, thus the saying: there is no war until brother fights brother. At the heart of this phenomenon lies every ethnic group's need to establish and maintain its identity as permanently and firmly as possible. Painstaking skill is required to distinguish yourself from those who resemble you. This is accomplished by the members of one ethnic group projecting onto the members of another ethnic group all that is negative in themselves that they do not wish to acknowledge as part of themselves. The ideal object for this projection is not someone whose characteristics are quite different from ours, but someone who is similar to us—just like us, and yet different.

It is a well-known fact that truth is the first victim of every war. Victory in the media war today is a prerequisite for any other kind of victory. The chapter "The Boomerang of Impassioned Bias" analyzes the social-psychological effects of spreading lies about oneself and one's enemies, and shows that the propaganda war unexpectedly inflicts considerable ("collateral") damage on any side that excessively aggrandizes its own group without reason and speaks ill of the members of other ethnic groups.

Prewar Sarajevo has been widely described as a town in which members of different ethnic groups—in particular the Bosnian Muslims, the Serbs, and the Croats— lived together in great love and harmony. The chapter "Endemic and Epidemic Ethnonationalists" classifies the forms of relationships that the members of each ethnic group in Sarajevo had with "the others" in the period between the formation and disintegration of the second Yugoslavia (1945–1991). Sarajevo, just as other environments, had its core of endemic nationalists; when the proper conditions had been met, ethnonationalism expanded from this core, taking on epidemic proportions.

Belittling others and aggrandizing one's own is a basic characteristic of ethnonationalism. The fact that ethnonationalism can be demonstrated paradoxically both as hatred towards one's own folk, along with a completely uncritical attitude towards the ethnonationalism of the community with which one's people are in conflict, is discussed in the chapter "Inverse Ethnonationalism."

During ethnic times the fate of mixed marriages (i.e., spouses from different ethnic groups) and the children of these unions is particularly difficult. The chapter "The Woes of Divided Loyalty" sheds light on different aspects of national and ethnic affiliations. Contrary to the claim of ethnonationalists, children from inter-ethnic marriages are not an ethnic anomaly. Their freedom to choose their ethnic group negates the rigidity of the basic ethnonationalist principle of strict and permanent divisions between ethnic groups.

All ethnonationalists argue that essential, insurmountable differences exist between the members of different ethnonational groups. Since biological differences are the easiest to show and prove, and since they are more durable than social-cultural differences, ethnonationalists are quite fond of the idea of the biological determination of their specific features. "Ethnonationalism in the Genes" presents arguments against such ideas.

The chapter "Brief Conversation with an Ethnonationalist about Children from Ethnically Mixed Marriages" describes some almost humorous aspects of ethnonationalists' bias. Ethnonationalism is a collective phenomenon. In other words, a very large number of people in areas under the sway of ethnonationalism share the same ethnonationalistic feelings and ideas. The collective nature of ethnonationalism is the basic reason why it is not a pathological occurrence. The concept of the (psycho)pathological is linked to individual existence and its specific bio-psycho-social features. Numerous misunderstandings would be avoided if a clear distinction were made between the concept of "disturbance" as a metaphor for highly different social phenomena and its use in the technical-psychiatric sense. The chapter "Is There Something Mentally Wrong with Ethnonationalists?" analyzes the differences between the collective, seemingly pathological, behavior of ethnonationalists and the individual psychopathological occurrence of ethnonationalism.

It has been noted that the transition period in Yugoslavia was marked by a rise in violence. So were ethnic times. Ethnonationalism was and still is a powerful generator of violence. Ethnonationalistic feelings and views encourage aggressiveness; when a target has been chosen, aggression is hastened. Sooner or later ethnonationalism leads to violence. Why and how? That is the topic of the chapter entitled "Why Ethnonationalists Are Aggressive."

In ethnic times, a disproportionately small number of people manage to resist the appeal of ethnonationalism, which has a hold over laymen and professionals alike. With their descriptions of the specific ethnonational traits of the Serbs and the Croats, Croatian and Serbian psychiatrists contributed to the general ethnonationalistic mood that has been so characteristic of a great deal of the Balkans in the past decade as described in the chapter "Ethnic Stereotypes in the Writings of Croatian and Serbian Psychiatrists."

How can one show and prove ethnic affiliation? Since ethnic origin is a key category in ethnic times, it should be easy to recognize a person's ethnic affiliation. This, however, is not the case. A person's looks, language, and even name do not necessarily reveal ethnic affiliation. Only better acquaintance, which most often means longer acquaintance, can help in guessing a person's ethnic identity. This is one of the paradoxes of ethnonationalism: ethnic singularity, the cornerstone of the whole idea of ethnonationalism, cannot be quickly and simply shown and proved. And it can also be hidden as discussed in "Prove You're a Serb."

In "Reactive Ethnonationalists," I consider the phenomenon of trying to find an explanation and justification for one's own ethnonationalistic feelings and views in the ethnonationalistic statements and behavior of "others." Those who advocate this kind of rationalization, assuming they are sincere, reduce themselves to passive beings and refuse any attempt to form their own opinion about their "own kind" and "other kinds."

Finally, the chapter "Obsession with Ethnicity" discusses my experience with the place of ethnicity or the ethnonational in people's lives based on my visit to Sarajevo in the summer of 2000, five years after the end of the war in Bosnia and Herzegovina. It was shown once again that the level of collectivization of individual existence—man the individual, disappearing behind the ethnonational group to which he belongs—is an indicator of the predominance of cultural over civil, ethnic over political.

Ethnic Times, I feel, is the most suitable title for this volume since the ethnic affiliation of people in what was once Yugoslavia has become a crucial factor. It determines whether a person will lose his/her life or be spared, whether a person will be fired or hired, whether a person will stay where he or she has lived until now or be forced to leave. As it has several times in the past, ethnicity clearly determines people's fate in the Balkans. In closing, I wish to thank Mrs. Alice Copple-Tosic, who translated the text from Serbo-Croatian.

Between Old and New Regimes

A psychiatrist's office greatly resembles the mirror held by Shakespeare's actors on the road of life. This is why psychiatrists are among the first to feel when an important disturbance is about to take place in society and among people. And when changes in the social environment become obvious, psychiatrists are able to monitor first-hand how they are reflected in people's views, feelings and, ultimately, in their behavior.

In the former Yugoslavia, at the very end of the 1980s and the beginning of the 1990s, it was not hard to notice that people who were not mentally disturbed often turned to psychiatrists for help. They came for advice, wanting to understand why they suddenly felt powerless, anxious. They wanted to go on sick leave, hoping to take refuge in the privacy of "illness" until "all of this" passed and they saw how it turned out. They asked if it were possible to take early retirement "because of their nerves," intending to withdraw from professional and even social life because "this was not their time." Some were even convinced they were really sick; they reasoned that one could only be crazy when the times were crazy. Some crossed the threshold of the psychiatrist's office seeking professional confirmation that they were mentally sound, which was basically intended to corroborate their intrinsic belief that it was the others who were crazy.

Listening to these people and observing them both inside and outside the psychiatrist's office, I tried to form a typology of individual patterns of behavior in this environment within that period of time. People's attitude towards the regime seemed to be the most natural criterion or crux upon which to classify different patterns of behavior. Ultimately, the change in the regime marked everything that happened in those years. The great change was a line of demarcation, a phenomenon that one had to come to terms with, if for no other reason than because the change, with its numerous expressions and consequences, was impossible to avoid. Finally, it was clear that even the lack of either an apparent or real attitude towards the change in the regime was nonetheless some sort of attitude and could not be accepted as mere indifference.

The following list of the most characteristic types of behavior is not based on their importance or frequency.

First type. People in this group had been openly committed to serving the previous regime and were either its protagonists or its executors. These people exhibited three main patterns of behavior in the newly arising circumstances. Some accepted the role of political has-beens calmly and rather stoically, following the logic: our time has passed; what we had is over; things must be accepted as they are; it's time to leave the social-political stage. The second group had trouble reconciling itself to the change and expressed disagreement and even some sort of rebellion by disparaging and besmirching the representatives of the new regime, loudly expressing doubts about their abilities and honesty. The third group was silent, refraining from any sort of commentary or evaluation of anyone or anything. Members of this group secretly hoped that their role in the old regime and the services they had provided would be quickly forgotten, thereby gaining (un)deserved benefit for themselves and their families. They had a vivid memory of the substantial number of people whose behavior during World War II had been less than honorable and who still received enviable positions in the new regime, now the old regime. They did not see why the new regime should be any different in this regard.

Second type. These people looked pragmatically at themselves and any circumstances in which they happened to be at any moment. They had served the old regime in a less intensive and less public manner than those in the previous group. Now, they were offering the same services to the new regime. They reasoned that there is salvation (and often pleasure) in serving and that all power is God-given. All regimes greatly rely on the work and skills of people with such views of the nature of social power and those who currently wield it. Characteristically, most people of this type do not verbalize their views about any regime, or at least not too publicly. They consider this improper and unwise. They have higher esteem—for themselves and for other people, as well as for consistency in maintaining the prescribed pattern of behavior towards those who are navigating the ship of state at any given time, regardless of where they are taking it, how skillfully and for how long.

Third type. These were people who did not offer the old regime much support, either openly or in secret, and spoke very little in favor of its unity and greatness. They rarely offered spontaneous support and primarily did so at the behest of representatives of the regime on very specific occasions. The old regime, for its part, repaid them in the same modest way, rewarding these people through social promotions and other customary compensation. These people had neither a love nor a hate relationship with the old regime; rather they had a mutual tolerance that turned more easily into animosity, on either or both sides, than into even the slightest cordial and intimate relationship. Should any of these people make a sudden dash for the regime, intending to stay there, the general view was that such a person's place had never been among the members of this vaguely defined group of people who knew each other for the most part, either by sight or reputation, and who clearly felt strongly about their attitude towards the regime—which might be described as going halfway.

A substantial number of these people greeted the new regime with no desire to cultivate the same relationship they'd had with the old regime. They were distrustful and reserved. Inwardly bolstered by some sort of self-sufficiency, they looked upon the new power holders with a mild feeling of superiority, forecasting that their turn at the helm would be rather short. They emphasized more than before the meaning and value of holding onto their moderately independent position towards any sort of external force which, by nature, could not keep account of anything individual, either individual people or their individual values.

Fourth type. These people have always considered that every regime is dirty and that only politics is dirtier. The end of an old regime and the emergence of a new one provides them with a unique opportunity to gloat, since such social turning points prove them to have been quite right to distance themselves from the old regime; power does not go without its flip side. There are never more insults, disparagement, empty promises, and manipulation of people as during the turning point when a new regime has just arrived and the old has not yet withdrawn completely. People of this type are always on the fringe of the social and political scene. Those who are at its center consider type-four persons highly destructive, which has never had much of an effect on this type.

Fifth type. These are people who are quite removed from the old regime. They could never forgive the old regime for the loss of their dear ones, the loss of material goods, or the loss of opportunities to properly show their abilities and worth. These people did not like the old regime because they could not, or dared not, openly express their beliefs and satisfy some need or other. A distinguishing characteristic of the new regime is that it promises or realistically creates conditions that will provide these people with satisfaction, enabling them to promote themselves in a way they could not in the old regime. Some people from the fifth-type group greet the new regime with unhidden sympathy, stressing that at least one thing is certain: the new regime cannot be worse than the old regime. Others, borne along by conscious or unconscious feelings of resentment, join the first ranks of the new regime, determined to rectify in the fastest and most radical manner that which they believe to have been wrong with the old regime. Such people are known to be quite impatient and militant, perhaps fearing that this chance, which they like to call historic, might slip by them. They are a type of (new) partisan.

Sixth type. These people, along with their families, suffered under the old regime more seriously than those from the fifth group. What both groups have in common is that they opposed and broke the laws and norms of the old regime, and were therefore punished in various ways. People from this group, and many other members of society, consider it quite natural for these sufferers to take over the new regime, or at least be in its immediate vicinity. It is not the least bit circumstantial that many members of the new regime's highest bodies have spent longer or shorter periods of time in prison in the recent and/or distant past. With few exceptions, the most prominent representatives of the old regime also had a prison record, particularly in the old regime's early years. The only difference, perhaps, lies in the fact that having a prison record in the old, now quite ancient, regime was stressed much more openly than today as one of the new cadres' strongest references (recommendations). We recall public announcements when "cadres" were appointed and decorated; their sojourns in prison, in a regime that had been against the interests of the people, were given a prominent place. The longer the prison term, the better. Those who recently took the reins of power are much less proud of the time they spent in prison. Inwardly they probably consider that the old regime was not so much against the interests of the people as the ancient regime had been in the eyes of those who are part of the old regime today.

Seventh type. These people who seem to make up the largest number became accustomed to the old regime during its four and a half decades of rule; the regime simply became part of their lives, with all its expressions and phases. At times they saw its advantages, at others they considered it an obstacle to the satisfaction of some need. At times they felt close, even very close, to the old regime, while at other times they felt alienated. It depended on what they wanted or were seeking from the old regime and themselves at any given moment. Outside their circle of like-minded thinkers (read: people of the same ethnic affiliation), these people do not want to announce whom they have voted for. First, overcome by sentimentality and despair, they console themselves that probably not much will change. Then they express impatience and ask why this better tomorrow hasn't arrived yet. Next, having decided to be practical, they contemplate how they can profit more from the new regime than the old. Finally, rather philosophically, they sum up the current situation and come to the conclusion that the only certain thing is great uncertainty.

We would be wrong to look through a prism made of moral principles at people whose everyday behavior more or less approximates the described patterns, and thereby praise them or find fault with them. We must not forget that people's general behavior, including their attitudes towards the old and new regimes, primarily stems from their temperament, their nature, and certainly from their personality, which is biologically preordained in part and partially formed in the process of maturation and one's upbringing. People are neither better nor worse than they might be. Fortunately or unfortunately, they are mostly the same. All that differs is their type (behavior). And perhaps in crucial moments, when regimes change, even their behavior is the same.

Why There Are so Many Faithful

In the 1980s, in the former Yugoslavia, people showed an intense need for faith and belief. Why was that? Behind every kind of fervor lies belief that there is salvation in our own kind, that only our ethnonational movement can bring all of us a better tomorrow, that only God can save us, that it is not a time for faithlessness. When one believes, it is in hierarchically higher values that tend to represent group, rather than individual, values. As a rule, one believes in something that surpasses reality, goes beyond it.

Faith is not of this moment; it is turned towards the future. It is indeed possible to believe in values that were part of the past. However, by bestowing our belief upon them we advocate their existence; we state our conviction that the best thing would be to reestablish those very same past values not only in the present but in the future, as well.

Faith is the offspring of deprivation. It is born and thrives where reality is cramped; thus, people try to step beyond the boundaries of reality through faith. Poverty has an overwhelming amount of faith. If abundance has faith, its strength cannot be measured against the faith of people who are destitute, particularly people who once lived in abundance.

Since faith, by its very nature, aims beyond what really exists, faith is the negation of reality. Faith is also promise. Promise cannot exist without faith. Faith never takes us all the way to what has been promised. There are beliefs whose advocates do not accept that they can only approach the object of their faith quite rarely, only during exceptional moments. Some beliefs want to self-destruct as quickly as possible so there is no longer any need for faith (i.e., for deprivation). Such beliefs actually do not need faith.

For faith to exist, criticism must be toned down. Faith does not grow in the proximity of doubt, the younger sister of disbelief. Faith exists because of the desire to believe or the need to believe and not because reason commands it. There are no believers among the overly rational. Someone once said that dreams are physiological insanity. Faith is not a dream, but it is closer to dreams than to reality. When a man ceases to believe as strongly or ceases to believe at all, the period when he was in the thrall of faith seems to him like a dream.

This brief account of some of the characteristics of faith should help us answer the question. Why did people have such a need to believe, at the end of the 1980s and in the 1990s, in what Yugoslavia and the countries that formed the region, were after its disintegration? In fact, faith was also to be found in the previous four or five decades in former Yugoslavia, even more at the beginning than near the country's end. There had been faith among the protagonists of the regime at that time, and among those who sincerely supported the regime. Those marginalized in Tito's Yugoslavia, more for political than social and economic reasons, had not lost faith either. It seems, however, that there was less faith during that entire period than there was during the transition, when the old regime was fading and the new one was still indistinct in many respects.

During the transition period faith became a truly basic need. Why? Because the system of values that had existed for many years was drastically disturbed. The pendulum of history began to swing wildly, and no one knew when, how, or where it would stop. Those who tried to orient themselves by holding to the rule that today is the opposite of everything that happened yesterday, lost their way in a twinkling. The signposts had faded so much they were illegible or else had been destroyed, and even the roads had ceased to be what they once were. The deprivation was complete and the uncertainty even greater. Asked about his own future and that of his near and dear, a man with any sense shrugged his shoulders, unable to answer. Fear of the unknown, fear of separation, fear-warning and fear-defense could be recognized in people's eyes and movements. When the future's dimensions are constricted to the limits of today, we turn to faith; for faith in tomorrow includes today, and often emphasizes what lies beyond—over what is on this side. Faith is the fulcrum we seek, the attempt to stand up straight today for tomorrow.

Since faith itself is more important than the object of faith, people have lots of faith in all kinds of things. Nonetheless, looking at the people around us, we can recognize a certain link between the preferred objects of faith and the circumstances that have produced such a need for faith and belief. When there is no semblance of order, when everything is unclear, little effort is needed to believe in someone who simplifies reality by reducing it to several dimensions which are ostensibly so important that compared to them all the rest of the multicolored world seems unimportant. If, in addition, the prime believer professes his faith ardently, with deep conviction, he must be believed.

Faith can be for oneself, and in oneself, alone. Most beliefs, however, presuppose not only a community of believers but also the profession of belief as a group, because there is special strength in strong group affiliation. Uncertainty pales in a group, political party, crowd, or procession, and the fears that individuals have brought with them are projected onto some other group now recognized as the enemy. In the group, in the collective, we know what we are supposed to do—as long as we believe.

The acceptance of religious precepts, which is only one form of faith, is first and foremost a type of pledge and confirmation of ethnonational identity. The public expression of religious beliefs and the increasing number of people taking part in religious rites is intended to fulfill many needs. It is intended to provide a new scope of orientation since what was in effect until yesterday has disintegrated, to serve towards the establishment of continuity (values, customs, etc.) at a time when discontinuity is the fundamental determinant of overall social happenings, to provide group affiliation, and so on. At a turning point, implied or detected continuity and powerful identification with an ethnic group offered guarantee of tranquility and security. It is therefore not coincidental that, by and large, the greatest number of political parties founded at turning points are ethnonational, and their members—and particularly their party leaders, with rare exceptions—actively participate in religious rights. They set a good example, one might say.

How authentic the current tide of religiousness is, how much of this greater participation in religious rituals results from the close connection between ethnic affiliation and religion among the Balkan peoples, and the degree to which this seeming rise in religiousness is nothing other than the expression of people's need to believe during times of transition, is, however, hard to tell.

Journey Through Post-Yugoslavia States in the Height of Ethnic Times

I left Sarajevo at the beginning of August 1992. At that time the town had already been without water and electricity for more than three months. There were shortages of everything, food most of all. The last three weeks before I left, my daily food allowance consisted of two or three sardines from a can and five or six slices of bread.

After the siege of Sarajevo that began on April 6, 1992, I went to my job at the Psychiatric Clinic in Kosovo General Hospital every day. I did not take the normal route I had taken during my 23 years of employment in this health care institution, but a roundabout way through streets that seemed less exposed to direct hits from the Serbs' artillery located on the hills around the city. The government had ordered all those who were employed on the eve of warfare to continue with their jobs. This was called a work obligation. I did not find this obligation difficult; since the month of May, when my wife and two daughters left Sarajevo, I had found it very hard to be alone. In addition, a tank truck supplied the hospital with small amounts of water so I could drink as much tea as I wanted, a habit that was harder to give up than going without food. To make the tea, I would dip cotton wool in spirit alcohol and then light it. There was enough heat to boil a liter or two of water, and I still had sufficient reserves of Earl Grey tea.

I hesitated a long time before leaving the city. Even though completely new rules of behavior had been quickly established in town; even though the city was run by local warlords and their brotherhoods, mostly people from the underground and almost every one with a thick criminal record; even though life in Sarajevo was becoming more difficult with each passing day, with the constant danger of losing one's life or being maimed by a sniper bullet or artillery shell; during the first months of the war I could not get rid of the conviction and feeling that Sarajevo was my town, and that my place was in my town. Then certain events that were of seemingly little importance indicated that I might not be completely right, that Sarajevo might not be my town any more. I recount here only three experiences that were greatly symbolic for me.

One morning in May when I arrived at work, I found the door to my office wide open. Someone had used considerable force to break it down since the door frame was seriously damaged. Once inside my office I established that nothing had been taken; nothing was even out of place. So, I thought, whoever broke in was not after something from my office. The broken door had more symbolic meaning. It was a warning. A message had been sent to me. The director of the clinic did not react to my request for an investigation to clarify the matter. The majority of my fellow psychiatrists passed over this incident in silence, as though nothing had happened. It was a time in which the unusual had become extremely habitual.

Most of the telephone lines in town had been cut off at the end of April. Only two or three telephones were still working in the entire hospital and, naturally, there was a line in front of each of them. One of the phones that still worked was located at the reception counter in the Infectious Clinic, quite close to the Psychiatric Clinic. Before using the phone, one had to write down in a notebook his/her name, as well as the name of the place he or she intended to call. I used that phone on several occasions. The first time I was truly bothered by the fact that the armed porter entered the telephone booth with me, and stayed with me during my conversation. The second time, standing in line, I noted that the armed porter went only rarely into the booth with those who had enough patience to wait for their turn. Finally, during my third or fourth time in line I tried to figure out which individuals were "privileged" to have the armed porter witness their telephone conversations. Since I knew most of the people in line personally, it was not hard to conclude rather quickly that the armed porter only listened to the conversations of those who were of Serbian ethnic origin. When my turn came, I asked the porter to leave the booth while I talked. He answered roughly that my use of the phone depended solely on his volition, and that if his presence while I talked bothered me I didn't have to use the phone at all.

During the first months of the war, I happened to spend a lot of time outside the clinic with Osman Djikic, a Bosnian Muslim, who had been the second Yugoslavian ambassador to Algeria and Finland. Osman was a broad-minded, well-read, cosmopolitan man, and an exceptionally valued conversationalist. At that time Sarajevo was criss-crossed with checkpoints. Each was guarded by an armed young man from the local neighborhood. He would check the identity of all passersby, and it was up to him whether a person was allowed into "his" territory. One early June afternoon, Osman and I were drawing near Kosovo Hospital. At a routine checkpoint, the man on duty asked for our identity cards. Osman's was given back to him at once, with a benevolent smile and thank you, which for these sentries, who are usually gruff and full of themselves, was quite unusual. He looked at my identity card for a very, very long time and then started to ask questions that were clearly answered by my identity card: date and place of birth, address, and so on. After this lengthy "double check," he returned my identity card without a word, looking at me quite unpleasantly. I could tell that Osman felt very uncomfortable about the whole thing. The reason for this difference in treatment was clear to both of us. I was born in Belgrade, and my first and last name clearly indicated that I am a Serb. The sentry wanted to let us know in the most obvious manner which one of us was welcome and which was not.

When I decided to leave Sarajevo, I was convinced that I would return very soon—in a few weeks, at most a month or two. I needed to believe that. Had I even suspected or dared accept the possibility that my departure might be final, I don't believe I would ever have left Sarajevo, although the city was becoming increasingly alien, distant. I remember that when I left my apartment at dawn on August 13, 1992, carrying just one bag, I had not thought it necessary to straighten up my desk even as much as a person who was leaving for a month.

During Sarajevo's almost four years of siege it was extremely difficult to leave the city, except for those who had the blessing of the Sarajevo government. To this very day it is inexplicable why the town's Bosnian Muslim government was so persistent in its refusal to let those who wanted to leave the city—if for no other reason than to feed fewer rather than more inhabitants in a situation when every loaf of bread was precious. People who could not understand the behavior of the Bosnian Muslim authorities said that Sarajevo was doubly surrounded: from the inside by the Bosnian Muslims, who would not let anyone leave the city, and from the outside by the Bosnian Serbs. Looking back, the explanation closest to the truth is that the international media's attention was as great as the suffering of the people in the besieged city. Reports from the international media inside the besieged city were expected to encourage international military action against the Serbs. If the Bosnian Muslim authorities in Sarajevo had allowed everyone to leave the city who wanted to, or assisted them in this regard, it was highly likely that an extremely large number of people would have left—in any case far more than the number that managed to leave with all the prohibitions and obstacles. Without most of its inhabitants, the city would have been of no interest to the media, reducing the hope that the countries of Western Europe and North America, pressured by voters' public opinion, would decide in favor of military action against the Bosnian Serbs. So the city became a twofold victim—of those who were systematically destroying it with mortars from the surrounding hills, and of those who held power in the city.

When I started on the road from Sarajevo to Belgrade to join my wife and children, my brother, and my sister, who had lived there with her family for a long time, I decided not to go through territory controlled by the Bosnian Serbs, although that was by far the shorter route. There were two reasons for not going through territory controlled by the Bosnian Serbs. First, I was enormously angry with the people who were destroying Sarajevo and its inhabitants, and I was horrified at the possibility of encountering them, even briefly. Second, I knew the Bosnian Serbs looked askance at my brother; at the very beginning of the war he had been a member of the Bosnia and Herzegovina presidency, which was considered by the Bosnian Serbs to be Muslim and not Serb controlled. Thus, they viewed presidency members as traitors, or, at the very least, of having sold their souls. Since my brother, his son, and I are the only ones with the surname Kecmanovic in Bosnia, and since I was not unknown to the public, I was afraid I might have great difficulties were I to take the route through the part of Bosnia controlled by the Serbs. Finally, I was not sure whether someone might tell Radovan Karadzic, a fellow psychiatrist with whom I had worked at the Psychiatric Clinic for more than ten years, that I was crossing this territory. Although I had not been in direct conflict with him in the years preceding the war, nor had any other colleague at the clinic, he knew perfectly well that I deeply disagreed with the policies of the political party he headed at that time; in other words, he and I were on opposite sides.

When I had managed to pass the checkpoints around the town—thanks to my sister-in-law, who was assistant editor-in-chief of the daily *Oslobodjenje* (one of a small number of Serbian journalists who remained loyal to the government in Sarajevo)—and reached Stup, a small town on the periphery of Sarajevo, it turned out that my fears about crossing territory controlled by the Serbs were justified. In order to reach the territory controlled by the Croats some fifty kilometers south of Sarajevo, I had to cross a narrow strip of one or two kilometers that was held by the Serbs. When they checked my identity at the entrance to this Serbian strip and saw my name, they told me I had to wait until they received authorization "from upstairs." I waited ten hours for that authorization in complete uncertainty, and then stopped waiting. In the end, a Serbian intelligence officer took me to Croatian territory for a few hundred German marks. I hitchhiked from the border to the town of Kiseljak and spent the night there with the brother of a colleague from the clinic, who was married to a Croat.

In the morning I obtained a permit to cross the territory of Herzeg-Bosnia, as the Bosnian Croat-controlled district of western Herzegovina was called at the time, and took the bus heading towards Split, a town on the Adriatic coast. During the second part of the trip, the bus took a winding road through the hills, climbing up towards Blidinjsko Lake above Jablanica. As we proceeded, the checkpoints became more frequent, and the police or soldiers who checked the passengers and their documents spent an increasing amount of time examining my permit to cross Herzeg-Bosnia and my identity card, asking more and more questions and becoming less and less willing to let me continue my trip. Finally, at the checkpoint on the large, dusty plateau where Blidinjsko Lake is located, what had been uppermost in my mind during the trip finally happened: They told me I could not continue my trip. All my pleadings and attempts at persuasion were in vain, including showing the letter from the Bosnian Academy of Science and Art that said that I was going to Zagreb, in conjunction with the Croatian Academy of Science and Art, to complete work on a two-volume encyclopedia of psychiatry. The bus stood there in the infernal heat as one of the military officers, who was clearly in charge, talked once, twice, three times over his walkie-talkie to someone I supposed to be his superior at one of the Herzeg-Bosnia centers. The result of these conversations was always the same. I could not continue on my trip. The other passengers' disgruntlement was almost palpable. Everyone wanted to reach their destination as soon as possible, and they were tremendously irritated by the delay caused by my "case." Their looks seemed to say: take your bag and go; let us continue on our way. At one moment I felt the soldiers' original determination to stop me from continuing my trip had slackened. I don't know why. They seemed to hesitate for a moment, grow weary or something. I took advantage of this moment and got on the bus, after which the driver quickly started the engine and we continued on our way.

Now I was a marked man. There was something wrong with me, with my documents. I was not to be trusted, unfit. There was no room for me in this bus or in the country of Herzeg-Bosnia. I felt the passengers staring at me with a mixture of curiosity and condemnation. I told myself over and over that things were fine, that I had been lucky with that one. I had no presentiment of the trouble I would soon encounter. On the way out of Posusje, as the bus was driving along a nice, wide, flat asphalt road towards Baska Voda, a small tourist spot on the Adriatic coast, a military police jeep overtook us and our driver was ordered to stop the bus. Two military policemen entered the bus and addressed the passengers, speaking almost in unison: "Which one of you is Dusan Kecmanovic?" I stood up. They motioned me to get out of the bus and to sit on the back seat of the jeep between two military policemen. The bus stayed there, and the jeep headed back to Posusje. I was soon inside the military police station. Across from me sat the commander of the military police, a large man with slow movements and an unpleasant expression on his face. He looked tired. What seemed to amaze and interest him most of all was how I, a Serb, would ever think of taking the route through Herzeg-Bosnia; even before this war it had been famous for its Croatian national-ist hardliners.

The hour-long interrogation was accompanied by his com-ments expressing great disdain for the Bosnian Muslims and their leadership, which I would say was even greater than his disdain for the Bosnian Serbs. When it was over he asked me whether I was aware that after the recent attack by Yugo (i.e., Serbian) aircraft on some places in Herzeg-Bosnia, they had decided to kill every Chetnik they got their hands on. I re-plied that I was not aware of such a decision and that I was not a Chetnik. The commander's comment was brief: "You are a Serb, so you are a Chetnik."

Just as he commanded his orderly to lock me up, a tall, rather thin young man entered the room wearing dark glasses and a dusty military police uniform. Later I realized that he was deputy commander of the military police. He sat across from me and asked quite coldly whether I still used Clan Aromatic pipe tobacco and whether I still drank Earl Grey tea. I was completely bewildered. The questions he asked told me I might not have to meet my maker after all, that my life might be spared. The man sitting across from me had to be someone who knew me from peaceful, civil times, someone who knew me well enough to know the type of to-bacco I smoked and the kind of tea I drank. This was what I had been missing most of all—some link to my earlier life, something or someone who would say loudly and clearly that

I was neither a Chetnik, nor a spy, nor an intruder, that I had done nothing to hurt anyone.

Every hope of salvation disappeared, however, when the newly arrived MP deputy commander asked me whether I had seen Miki Markovic recently. Miki Markovic had come to Sarajevo from Serbia a dozen years before. He worked in the administration office at the Psychiatric Clinic. What singled him out from most other people employed in the clinic, and from those in the hospital, was his more than aggressive admiration of Slobodan Milosevic, a man who had come to power in Serbia at the end of the 1980s. Miki aggrandized almost everything connected to the Serbian people with an open-heartedness that was unusual among long-time residents of Sarajevo, particularly with regard to the characteristics of specific ethnic groups and what the relationships among ethnic groups were or should be. He did it so often and in such a conspicuous manner that many believed he must have been a provocateur. When the MP deputy commander in Posusje, in the heart of Croatian nationalistic extremist country, asked me whether I had seen Miki recently, my newly raised hopes of salvation disappeared without a trace. Hesitating, I replied that I had seen him recently, but only just as much as my job required.

They told me to leave the room and sit on a bench in the hall. I don't know how long I sat there under the watchful eye of the guard at the entrance to the building. I could not hear the conversation between the commander and his deputy through the soundproof padding on the door. When the deputy commander finally appeared at the door, he told me to follow him. He put me in the seat next to him in a large Ford with a German license plate, and took me back towards the bus. That is when he introduced himself, and said he had been my student at the junior college medical school in Sarajevo. He had taken the oral examination before me, and had seen the tobacco I smoked and the tea I drank. Then, a little protectively, a little worried, he said, "I'm surprised at you, Professor; I thought you were an intelligent man. I can't understand how you as a Serb would go through Herzeg-Bosnia in such terrible times as these. If I hadn't appeared, they would certainly have killed you." Then he added, "I had open radio contact when those guys in the field passed on to the commander the wonderful news that they had caught a Chetnik, Dusan Kecmanovic. As soon as I heard that, I thought it must certainly be you, so I rushed to headquarters." I couldn't help asking him what his mention of Miki Markovic was supposed to mean. He replied that he'd shared accommodations with Miki Markovic for several years in Sarajevo. They'd become close friends and had spent great moments together; those had probably been the best years of his life. So he really did want to know what had happened to Miki. I thought to myself: such criss-crossed connections between people and their fate is only possible in Bosnia. And Herzegovina, of course.

There was no end to my amazement when we found the bus in the very same place it had been stopped by the military police more than two hours previously. I had the feeling that the passengers were not surprised to see me again. They seemed resigned to the situation. The rest of the trip to Split was calm.

In Split I spent the night at a friend's and went to the Psychiatric Clinic the next day. It's hard to say why I went to the clinic. It's true that I knew almost every psychiatrist at the clinic; some were also dear friends. But I was a refugee on the long and extremely uncertain road to Belgrade. It was wartime, I should have been on my way as soon as possible. What was I looking for at the Psychiatric Clinic? When I think about it all today, it seems to me that I went to the clinic in order to keep my professional and social identity from further deterioration, to show myself through my colleagues' attitude towards me that I was still something more than just a refugee, one of the hundreds of thousands who had lost their home, and their professional and social status. Nothing takes away a man's identity and makes him anonymous like the status of refugee. All refugees are the same, just as all inmates are the same. The previous profession, reputation, and property of refugees and inmates mean nothing; the future they once had no longer exists.

The director of the clinic in Split, Professor Borben Uglesic, received me with extreme kindness. He excused himself for not being able to provide me with accommodations as his brother and family, refugees from Dubrovnik, were staying with him. He suggested that the best way to go to Zagreb was to fly. On the way to the airport bus terminal, he asked me to wait while he went into a bank. When he returned he stuck an envelope of money into my pocket with the words, "That's my month's salary. Half for you, half for me. Just in case you need it."

When I arrived in Zagreb I went straight from the airport to the Psychiatric Clinic of Rebro General Hospital. I told Professor Jovan Bamburac I would be staying just a day or two until I found a way to go to Belgrade. He gave me his office, which contained a bed and shower in addition to a desk and bookshelves. I needed nothing more. I rarely went downtown during the two days I spent in Zagreb. They told me it would be better not to walk around town since the police frequently asked people for their identity cards, and I might run into trouble or even be summarily deported since I had no other document except my Yugoslav passport. It was no longer valid in Croatia, they said, and it was better not to show it. I went to the Croatian Academy of Science and Art, where the vice president of the Academy received me kindly and inquired about happenings in Sarajevo, in particular at the Bosnian Academy of Science and Art.

As I was sitting, or rather lying down, in Bamburac's office, in some sort of semi-space and semi-time, suffering from the unbearable lightness of being, a group of colleagues from Rebro Hospital came to visit. They appeared a little uncertain, even frightened, speaking in low voices. I quickly noted that they were all Serbs. They had come to visit their co-ethnic in ethnic times. They expressed concern about my fate, and it seemed to me that they were actually more concerned about their own. I must admit that all together they looked both funny and sad. From the very beginning of the 1990s when nationalist sentiments started to run high in all parts of the second Yugoslavia, then through the months of war spent in besieged Sarajevo, and finally after the experience of my trip until then, I had become extremely hostile to everything that was mono-ethnic. I could not feel any differently about the visit of my fellow Serbs from the Psychiatric Clinic in Zagreb, with all due respect for their attention and concern for me.

Professor Bamburac said he would go to the bus station with me. There was a bus line from Zagreb to a small town in Hungary, although I have forgotten the name. From there it was a kilometer or two on foot, and then another bus for Belgrade. As we approached the bus station, Bamburac told me it would be better if I went to the ticket window by myself. He explained that he was known to the public, that he had been on TV quite often of late, advocating, as a Serb, a peaceful solution to the highly intense conflicts between the Serbs in Croatia and the Croats. He felt it would be awkward if the clerk at the window were to recognize him as the friend of a man buying a ticket to Belgrade. To this very day I don't know whether he was exaggerating or whether there was any basis for his fear of being compromised. One thing is certain, though; he was a well-known public figure in Zagreb at the time. It was not hard to notice that quite a few people we passed on the street stared at him meaningfully. Instead of asking for a ticket to the small town in Hungary, I asked quite spontaneously for a ticket to Belgrade. The clerk was speechless. Her expression didn't even change. It was as though I hadn't said a thing. When I repeated my request, she just shook her head no. I realized immediately how big a mistake I had made, and walked away from the window confused and embarrassed. Bamburac was waiting for me at the exit to the bus station.

In order to spare my host and myself from further unpleasantness, I bought a train ticket to Budapest and left Zagreb the same night. After waiting several hours in Budapest, I continued by train to Belgrade. The following scene that occurred on the way from Budapest to Belgrade sticks in my memory. At the border, just after entering Serbia, a Serbian passport controller came into the compartment where I was sitting with a young man unknown to me. For the first time on my trip I felt no qualms about my personal documents. I was certain that this time I would not have to worry about my Yugoslav passport. It was still considered valid in Serbia and Montenegro. I must say it felt good to finally stop being a suspicious person, or so it seemed. I would not have to fear men in uniforms anymore.

This, I could see, was not the case with my silent fellow passenger, who had entered the train several stations before the border; his comportment told me that he was not in a mood to talk, which I had respected. When the Serbian policeman entered the compartment, my fellow traveler withdrew even more, and his behavior became even stiffer. Since he was sitting across from me I couldn't help noticing that he also had a Yugoslav passport. The policeman held it in his hand, looking at it carefully, and then asked the man where he was traveling to. There was no reply. The question was repeated in a much louder and openly menacing tone. I looked at the young man. His expression had not changed a bit. In psychiatric language, he seemed to be in some sort of semi-stupor. Then the policeman, filled with anger and aggressiveness, returned the man's passport with the words, "Ah, you don't understand Serbian. You'll learn, boy will you learn, all you Albanians. You'll learn Serbian; you'll learn to sing in Serbian." He left the compartment, slamming the door behind him.

In Belgrade, the tension that had been my companion for months relaxed for a moment. I was with my wife, my little girls, my brother, my sister. But even though the tension had relaxed very quickly and the voice of quiet despair inside me had retreated, I soon found myself in the claws of complete uncertainty with regard to my own future and the future of my children. There were worries about day-to-day survival and almost daily exposure to humiliations of the widest variety. The heads of numerous psychiatric institutions in Belgrade, who had been my personal friends for years, were not prepared to offer me even temporary employment. The reason they gave was an agreement with Radovan Karadzic, reached at the "highest level," to the effect that prominent Serbs from Bosnia and Herzegovina, were not to be given employment in Belgrade, thus forcing them to return to the part of Bosnia controlled by the Serbs to help their "brother Serbs."

There were actually numerous reasons for their refusal to give me a helping hand. All the heads of the psychiatric institutions in Belgrade were either members of the leading political parties in Serbia or supported by word and deed Milosevic's policies at the time. They had all without fail been informed of my views on the political leadership of the Bosnian Serbs, of my bitterness towards the actions of Serbian paramilitary units in the eastern parts of Bosnia, of what they regarded as my mondialistic a-national views. Finally, they feared (some of them said this openly, years later) that with my knowledge, professional competence, and the reputation I enjoyed among other psychiatrists, I might endanger them and disturb the order that they had established and carefully preserved.

One thing that never ceased to amaze me, and over time vexed me more and more in Belgrade, was a question asked by both friends and acquaintances. In a low voice, as though in confidence, they asked me, "Please tell us who is really bombing Sarajevo . . ." I simply could not believe that people in Belgrade did not know that the Serbs and the Serbs alone had been bombing Sarajevo night and day for the past six months. Was it that people, my psychiatrist colleagues above all, could not or did not want to look the truth in the eye, or had they been so deceived by the Serbian media's propaganda that they truly could not understand who had been destroying Sarajevo for months?

When the head of the Psychiatric Clinic in Belgrade invited me to the last meeting of the organizing committee of the Psychiatric Congress of Yugoslavia, which was to be held in Belgrade a few weeks later, I accepted. "Come to our Psychiatric Department in Avala. The food will be excellent," he said, explaining his invitation, and then added with a smile, "Refugees always clean their plates."

My financial situation did not make me immune to invitations of this type and, feeling rather professionally isolated all those months, I looked forward to the chance to meet a larger number of colleagues, the leaders of our profession. The chairman of the meeting, the director of the Psychiatric Clinic who had invited me, gave me the floor soon after the meeting began, saying that this was a unique occasion for them to hear first-hand about the state of psychiatric services in Sarajevo in conditions of war. I could not let this chance go by. I spoke of the suffering of the inhabitants of Sarajevo, of fellow psychiatrists and psychiatric patients. I said that the Bosnian Serbs' military forces had occupied Jagomir Psychiatric Hospital located on the outskirts of Sarajevo; they had dismissed the staff and discharged all the patients, most of them chronic mental patients who could not take care of themselves. I told them that these patients, completely abandoned and starving, were wandering through the streets of the town, increasing its ghostly appearance. Finally, I added that we as psychiatrists must condemn this criminal act. I spoke excitedly. When I was through, a long, rather unpleasant silence ensued. The chairman asked whether anyone had any questions or comments. No one said a word. An even greater, invisible barrier had been created between my colleagues and me. I was some sort of black sheep among them.

That night, from two in the morning until dawn, the telephone in the apartment we rented rang several times. When I lifted the receiver, no one answered, leaving the line open. The next day, as far as I remember, the decision to depart the post-Yugoslavia states reached a head. It was time to leave for distant parts.

Neither Sick nor Hale and Hearty

Confronted by phenomena that, to put it mildly, confuse them, many of those living in the countries formed after the disintegration of the second Yugoslavia wonder what has happened to people's mental health in these sinister times, in this era that is not an era. As is often the case when facing something that escapes the power of rationalization, people have found a general, universal explanation for all the irrational and unintelligible happenings, and particularly for the incomprehensible behavior of people around them: they are insane, mentally ill. This is followed by the conclusion that since the people around us are insane, it's no wonder that we have lost our minds. It turns out that Blaise Pascal's *dictum* can be perfectly applied to all of us: Men are so necessarily mad that not to be mad would amount to another form of madness.

Regardless of the relief brought by putting this label on the widest variety of phenomena and people, feeling that we have thereby explained them, it actually clouds the issue: What has happened to the mental health of our fellow citizens (and our neighbors, too)? Have they really lost their minds? Have circumstances made them this way, or has their madness, which used to be hidden, created these circumstances in order to allow them to feel more at ease?

Let me say straightaway that the people I see around me, in the street and at the speaker's podium in Parliament, do not seem mentally ill, at least in most cases. But are they mentally healthy? They would be if the fact that a person is not mentally ill were proof of his sanity. But it is not. The absence of illness is certainly a necessary but not a sufficient condition for someone to be mentally healthy.

Bearing this in mind, it should be noted that the concepts of the mentally healthy and mentally ill are extremely often misused for the widest variety of reasons. There are, however, two basic forms of misrepresenting soundness of mind: first, when mentally healthy is equated with the average state of mental health, and second, when the evaluation of someone's sanity is based on how much he has adapted his behavior and manner of thinking to the social (group, ideological, party, etc.) norm. Although seemingly different, both these definitions of mentally healthy have a lot in common and even complement each other, and both of them are wrong in many ways.

First, man's mental health, just like man himself, is a dynamic value, which means that a man cannot be defined by what he already is but by what he will be or might be. Any statement about man's present or man in the present, means the "average" present man as something greatly desirable and valuable (and soundness of mind is most certainly a desirable value); however, this means taking away man's future, that is, his very self.

Second, it is no less dangerous to link soundness of mind to any sort of social program or norm. Being mentally healthy cannot only mean being what is socially acceptable and desirable; all groups, all societies, all collectives (organization, party, society) try to reach the point where their members ardently want what best suits the interests of the collective. In other words, there will always be antagonism between individually and socially structured soundness of mind.

That the above definitions of mentally sane are unfounded becomes more than obvious when applied to the circumstances that prevailed in the second Yugoslavia during the last years of its existence and in most states that were formed after its disintegration. How did most people act, what did they do, how did they think—in other words, what happened to the average man in these countries at that time? Most people contributed to the current state of affairs, which is far from desirable, with their voting ballots. Furthermore, they allowed a small number of people with little intelligence and great greed to manipulate them as much as they wanted, whenever they wanted. They went along with the idea that they should hate, persecute, and kill their former neighbors, which they never would have done by themselves because they did not have sufficient reason. Their living standard is plunging, and the future, in realistic terms, hasn't the slightest rosy tinge.

Of course, from the viewpoint of those in power, most people's behavior, manner of thinking, and feeling, are desirable. It is the expression of people's political maturity, and the fact that their eyes have opened in the political sense, that they have finally started to think with their own heads. Not much effort is required, however, to understand that most people's attitude towards themselves and the world has little in common with soundness of mind.

Sanity is an individual-psychological, as well as universal, category. It is individual-psychological insofar as it is the individual who is mentally healthy (or ill, as the case may be); it is universal because mental health cannot be linked to any social-political program or standard. There has been one other attempt to trivialize soundness of mind, which means to compromise it. This is the not uncommon case of considering a man mentally healthy if he feels satisfied, if he is at peace with himself. We should not forget, however, that people feel self-satisfied primarily when what they want out of life is in keeping with what life offers them. This definition of soundness of mind is unacceptable primarily because what life can offer a man at any given moment often greatly depends on external circumstances upon which the individual has limited influence; thus he or she has little chance of being able to thank or to blame for his/her own happiness. (The exceptions, of course, are people who are always happy, regardless of the circumstances and how much they can influence them; a large number of such people can be found in the population of the mentally underdeveloped.) Finally, this definition of mentally sane means, inter alia, that we will provide, preserve, or even reach soundness of mind if we lower the level of our aspirations a little bit every day—if we want, look for, and expect less and less out of life as time goes by.

What then is soundness of mind? I will try to answer this question indirectly. Roughly speaking, man is exposed to two kinds of pressures: internal and external. Internal pressures can be conscious and unconscious. Unconscious pressures are usually more intense. They originate in unresolved personal conflicts and surface in the form of fear, dissatisfaction, feelings of deprivation, aggression, and so on. Everyone has internal conflicts; the only difference from person to person is the dominant type of conflict and its intensity.

In addition to internal pressures that are connected to the individual and ensue from the dynamics and manner of his/her development, everyone is influenced by pressures inherited as a member of a specific collective. The individual is only partially aware of these pressures; that is, he or she does not always experience them as pressures, or is not at all aware of them. They are reflected in specific views, beliefs, regulations, prohibitions—thus the entire normative framework of the collective (family, tribe, community, etc.) to which the individual belongs. In the broader sense, this normative framework of the collective includes collective notions, which are the collective's perceptions about its "natural" and "unnatural" friends and enemies, about the dominant and defining characteristics of its members and the members of other collectivities.

Regarding the external pressures that the individual is exposed to, it should be noted that a good share of the internal pressures, both those from the personal and from the collective unconscious, started out as external pressures. Through the process of upbringing and education they were gradually internalized and became a component of the individual's psychological profile, his/her behavior, beliefs, reasoning, and attitude towards himself/herself and others.

Since the times in which we live are ruled by the ethnonational collective, I would say that the intensity with which someone states and advocates the views and beliefs of an ethnonational group testifies, among other things, to the intensity of the pressure formed by the spirit of that collective, regardless of how much the individual feels compelled to act in accordance with the dictates of the ethnonational group. Where ethnonational communities are in open conflict with each other there is additional identification with the ethnonational collective, once again owing to pressure. The pressure is external since the collectives, the communities in conflict, do not tolerate indecision; they seek clear and incontrovertible lines that separate them. (Conflicting collectives are mostly exclusive collectives.) On the other hand, the pressure is also internal, since identification with the collective is experienced internally as a way to gain the strength and power of the collective (my people stand behind me). Added to this, a number of internal pressures linked to personal conflicts and feelings of deprivation can be seemingly resolved by renouncing one's own individuality and blending into the collective. It is therefore clear why so many people cannot resist the pressures of the collective and fall prey to it.

Man cannot escape either internal or external pressures. They are a component of his/her life. Furthermore, one of the things that differentiates one person from another is how much he or she yields to those pressures. Since man is far from being just a passive creature, the degree of a person's mental health can be measured by how much he or she has remained or become a prisoner of these conscious and unconscious, internal and external pressures, and how much he or she can reduce their hold and oppose them. To be more exact, mental health can be measured by how successful an individual is in not letting external pressures, without which there is no socialization, and internal pressures, without which it is hard to imagine individual life, stand in the way of achieving his inherent developmental potentials, of realizing himself as a creative and self-creating being.

Now we seem to be closer to answering the question asked at the beginning of this chapter: How mentally sane or mentally disturbed are people in the areas of former Yugoslavia? We will be even closer to the answer if we accept that sanity is not a clearly bounded entity, that it is most accurately presented as a dimensional or continual value. Imagine a line with mentally sane at one end and mentally ill, mentally disturbed at the other. There is almost no one at either of these poles, and each of us, at different periods in our lives and in different living situations, is closer to or farther from these extreme points of the imaginary dimension of mental sanity–insanity. To this I would add that a classification of the *degree* of sanity should be constructed. Just as there are many mental diseases, different mentally ill states that are more or less strictly separate entities, there are also different forms or degrees of mental sanity.

Medical experts, as a rule, have a hard time coping with different forms of exhibiting sanity. Since they are primarily experts for illness, and only secondarily for health, they are inclined to consider certain forms of mental sanity an expression of illness. So they invent different names for an allegedly sick state of mental health that is in essence only a special state of health. On an imaginary scale of mentally healthy–ill, roughly speaking, one-half of the scale would make up primarily pathological states and the other half primarily psychically normal states. Unaccustomed to health, doctors—psychiatrists, in particular—usually designate pathological states that take up far more than one-half of the imaginary mentally healthy–ill scale. This is why you will hear more than one doctor say that a considerable number of people are mentally disturbed today.

How can we finally determine the degree of someone's mental sanity? Since the type and degree of mental disturbance is based on what a person says and how they act, or how they experience themselves and the world around them, the degree of a healthy state of mind can be determined similarly. Let me mention several possible indicators of the state of someone's mental health:To what extent does the individual experience himself/herself as a subject, as the bearer of his/her own powers, activities, and abilities? To what extent can he or she objectively observe what is going on inside and around him/her? In other words, to what extent, under internal and external pressures, does he or she misrepresent reality in and around himself/herself? Furthermore, how does the individual feel or reason if, by a concurrence of events, he or she finds himself/herself in a completely new and different social environment? Broadly speaking, how functional is his/her behavioral pattern in an environment where the group, the collective upon whose dictates he or she has primarily adjusted his/her own behavior, no longer exists? Do internal and external pressures allow the individual to learn from experience, to reach objective (unbiased) conclusions from newly arising situations, from altered external circumstances? To what extent do internal and external pressures help or hinder the development of a man as an individual, stand in the way of or encourage his/her individualization and socialization, his/her personal growth and development?

If we were to try right now to answer the question about people's state of mental health at the end of the 1980s and in the 1990s in most of the territories of former Yugoslavia, we could say that they were neither sick nor hale and hearty. In other words, it seems that most people were not entirely sound of mind, that their mental sanity had dropped to a very low level. It goes without saying that the individual's personal freedom and his morale were in the same unenviable state.

The Violence of Daily Life

At the end of the 1980s and in the 1990s, violence became an important characteristic of daily life for people in most parts of the former Yugoslavia and the countries that were formed after its disintegration. There was no escaping violence; either you inflicted it or fell prey to it. There was no third possibility. What was behind this wave of violence? There were many causes and reasons, both direct and indirect, behind this wave of violence. I will point out in random order several that seem especially important.

Life Had No Normative Framework. Yesterday's written and unwritten rules and laws that regulated people's behavior in the community were no longer in effect. New rules and standards of behavior still had not taken root. During the transition period, the normative framework of life was not properly defined and was even contradictory. At the same time, there was no punishment for breaking the law, which meant that the normative framework could not carry out its basic function of guiding and restricting people's behavior.

Knowledge that breaking the old law, which was losing force or the new law, which had yet to be accepted by everyone, would go unpunished, removed the fear of repression and social reprisal that are greatly to be credited for what is called civilized behavior. If one of the essential factors that shape and maintain civilized behavior is missing, man more readily obeys the voice of the barbarian within him.

Role Models. Social behavior is learned or formed by imitating the behavior patterns that are offered to us when we are growing up or that we choose ourselves in conjunction with our proclivities, living circumstances, etc. The more attractive the role model, the stronger the imitation.

On the social scene during the last years of the second Yugoslavia and in the states formed after its disintegration, what was shown to be, and still is, the most attractive role model for a vast number of people? In the general breakdown, the individuals who attracted attention and prompted envy were those who imposed themselves by the strength of their authority, power, rapid acquisition of wealth, and disregard for anyone or anything; these were individuals who placed violence above honesty and respectability. Success, that magic word for most people, has never been so closely associated with depredation. It is almost impossible to find anyone today whose lifestyle indicates that a person can become rich, famous, and powerful, and still be honorable (the underprivileged, poor and powerless will find a nice alibi in this statement!). The immoral are becoming too strong to require an alibi.

Maladjustment. Things are happening today that people could never have imagined. Reality constantly eludes them because of the speed with which meanings change, far surpassing their powers of anticipation. There can be no question of adjusting to a reality that changes day after day. Circumstances simply have to stay more or less the same for a while in order for a person to adjust to them. A great part of our life consists of habits, which means our life proceeds according to the dictates of conditioned reflexes. We have learned to associate specific conditioned stimuli with the unconditional and with the satisfaction of different needs—some vital, some social. If reality and its symbols change rapidly, the conditioned stimuli change as well, which means that we cannot form habits known as second nature.

A person without habits is basically maladjusted, confused, disoriented, disturbed. Dissatisfaction and anger are inevitably directed at—what else?—such a reality, other people, their property, common goods. Everyone is to blame for the fact that we can't cope, are lost, and can't recognize each other, let alone our own selves. Finally, if social reality benefits man so little, it might as well not exist. For this reason it should be even more discredited, depersonalized, trampled, and destroyed—along with the people who are part of such a reality.

Frustration Everywhere. The surest way to make someone aggressive is to frustrate the satisfaction of his/her needs. The more frequent and complete the frustration, the greater the aggressiveness.

Today it is quite difficult to enumerate all the powers and circumstances that have interjected themselves between a person and the satisfaction of his/her extremely important needs, such as food, security, love, respect, and self-respect. When aggressiveness, or, if you will, the readiness to react aggressively, rises sharply, it no longer needs the stimuli that are normally linked with aggressive behavior. Quite unspecific stimuli are enough. Thus, you might lose your life simply because someone thinks you have looked at them askance.

Uncertain Future. Man's psychic energy is rallied by objectives, in particular by some long-term goal. For the sake of this goal we are prepared to put up with current misfortune, hold onto our composure and, in a word, persevere. When the future is uncertain (despite repeated assurances by those in power that it couldn't be rosier), the meaning of individual and collective exertions is brought into question. When individual and collective energy is squandered, deterring forces weaken, solicitude disappears, and violence becomes one of the fundamental forms of relating with other people and with reality in general.

The Only Certainty Is Uncertainty. If you are threatened on a daily basis with the danger of being insulted, physically injured, of being mistreated for hours by unknown people, or losing your life for no reason; if, after being absent for several hours or days you are not sure you will find your apartment intact and not robbed, then you are forced to spend an enormous amount of psychic energy on usually unsuccessful attempts to decrease the sources of such threats while keeping some sort of control over the fear that inevitably accompanies this uncertainty.

One of the direct results of lengthy, exhausting, and conscious or unconscious opposition to sources of internal and external threat is a decrease in the threshold of sensitivity to highly varied stimuli. When this threshold is greatly reduced—particularly if uncertainty is prolonged indefinitely and even increased—a person's activities and reactions are influenced less and less by reason and solicitude, and more and more by selfishness and momentary interest. Violence is a natural instrument with which to heed the dictates of selfishness, irrationality, instinctive drives, and the "language of blood."

Great Expectations–Great Disappointment. If you don't take something for granted (i.e., if you don't expect a certain sequence of events, behavior, etc.), you have safeguarded yourself against the possibility of being disappointed. Disappointment is simply the result of making a wrong judgment.

The new regime was the focus of great and sincere expectations. Today, several years after ethnonational parties won the elections, there is no end to the disappointment: the living standard is worse than before. A small group of people close to the government have become enormously wealthy, unemployment is high, a large number of people are barely surviving, and corruption is becoming more and more entrenched.

How can one cope with the bitter feeling of having been deceived? People are not inclined to be angry with themselves and are even less willing to accept that they themselves have made a mistake. On the other hand, in circumstances with a general ethnocentric orientation, it is hard for a person to accept that the promoters and mainstays of his/her own victorious ethnonational party have deceived him. What follows is an almost inevitable psychological maneuver: I am not the only one who has been deceived, but all my brothers and sisters by ethnic affiliation, as well. Who has deceived them, duped them, and led them out onto thin ice? The others, of course, those from another ethnic group, those from the rival or enemy ethnonational party. We are so disappointed and our expectations have been so greatly crushed that our revenge must be just as great. Those "others" must suffer.

Psychopaths. Psychopaths are a strange breed of people. They are both healthy and sick, and neither healthy nor sick. As a rule they are asocial, turned inward towards their own interests, with no consideration for other people. They have no feelings of guilt for the crimes they commit, and thus most cannot learn from experience. The attention psychopaths attract from those around them is commensurate with the frequency with which they disobey social norms. They are almost always in open or hidden conflict with their environment.

Because of their disregard for other people and for the rights and needs of others, during times of peace a number of psychopaths, particularly the highly asocial types, spend quite a lot of time either in jail or in a mental hospital or special institution. In chaotic times, their lack of socialization is less noticeable or even completely inconspicuous because there is widespread disrespect for the normative framework of life. Since they prove to be insensitive bullies and true thugs, during chaotic times psychopaths lead the way, gain recognition, arouse envy, and serve as role models. They have shown themselves truly irreplaceable in carrying out the ethnic persecution (read: cleansing) that has marked our era.

Ethnic Prejudices. Ethnic prejudices are rationally unfounded, negative views accompanied by strong emotions;

they are lasting judgments of the members of other ethnonational groups.

The function of almost all prejudices, including ethnic ones, is to justify certain exploitative relations, to satisfy various personal goals, desires (wealth, social standing, etc.) and even inclinations (greed, brutality, etc.), or to ensure acceptance in an environment where certain prejudices are widespread.

Regardless of what lies behind the individual's adoption of ethnic prejudices, having these prejudices means fostering an aggressive and disparaging attitude towards people from one or more quite specific ethnonationalities. Ethnonationalism is based on the conviction that something makes my people better, more worthy, more important than other peoples. Therefore, the members of my people have the right to expand at the expense of others, to impose their own system of values and beliefs, or to disassociate themselves from other ethnonational groups in order to protect themselves from the necessarily less worthy and often dangerous inclinations and customs of other peoples.

Those with ethnic prejudices voice an almost universal explanation—to themselves and others—for the hatred, aggressiveness, and deprecation that rules their relationship with members of another ethnonationality. We don't hate people from the other ethnonationality; rather they hate us, and our hatred is only a means to defend ourselves from their hatred. The mechanism at work here is projection, which means attributing to other people our own feelings, opinions, views. It is at the heart of every paranoid attitude.

All ethnonationalists are convinced that they were, are, and/or will be endangered by the members of other ethnonational groups. When one is convinced of this, all that remains is to find all possible means to restrict, vilify, drive out, and destroy the members of that ethnonational community and everything connected to it. Whether this is done as a deterrent or a reaction makes no difference.

Violence Is Its Own Justification. The belief is widespread that if a man is tense and angry for any reason he should get rid of his/her negative energy: yell at someone, hit someone, or break something—in short, "relieve" or "empty" himself of the aggression. We forget that whether or not a man is aggressive depends not only on his/her tenseness, anger, and negative emotions, but on what is in his/her head. Under the condition that a person is not morally defective, every time he or she seriously injures another person, he or she seeks justification for this violent, aggressive behavior. If a person is the slightest bit honest and decent—and each of us firmly believes we are—then he or she must first explain to himself why he or she robbed, hit, mutilated, or killed someone. In other words, if the victim is truly innocent, then a man has to convince himself/herself that the victim is not quite so innocent, despite evidence to the contrary. The more deserving the victim in the eyes of the perpetrator, the greater the violence, which is accompanied by more and more "proof" that the victim got what he deserved.

The End Justifies the Means. Many people believe that history is being made right now, and add that where history is being made there is violence. Hundreds and even thousands of dead, wounded, crippled have marked all turning points in history. What is worrisome in the Balkans is that quite a few people would like to make history primarily to become part of it. Another disturbing fact is the obvious and significantly large disproportion between loudly stated beliefs that those in power are fighting for great ideals and the considerable evidence that base interests are proving to be the true driving force behind their activities.

It is hard to say which source of violence is stronger in the Balkans: the delirious, enthralled, abusive creators of history or the primarily quiet multitude of people who have accepted, quite literally, the widespread opinion that revolutionary times are by definition brutal, and that during them almost everything is permitted. Revolutionary Machiavellianism,

history tells us, has always been broad enough to cover, as
well as hide, the work of countless swindlers, looters, and
murderers.

The Agony and the
Ecstasy of the Victim

I have been working in a private practice in Sydney for the past several years. A number of my patients are from the former Yugoslavia. I have the rare privilege of treating all three ethnonationalities (Serb, Croat, and Muslim) whose members, until recently, were waging terrible warfare, destroying each other.

Among the many similarities in the psychic disturbances that distress them, it is striking that all of these patients, without exception, see themselves as victims. And, of course, they are victims, forced to leave their homes and make their way in the wide world, most without any resources. But this is not what it's about. Members of all three ethnonational groups feel—or rather, are deeply convinced—that they and their ethnonational brothers and sisters are victims of the other two groups, both in peacetime and in wartime. What is particularly interesting is that each cites abundant proof that they and members of their ethnic group are truly victims—victims in the recent conflicts, in conflicts fifty, seventy years ago, in conflicts six centuries ago—without even mentioning their peacetime victimization. All in all, it turns out that for shorter or longer periods each was equally a victim. Common sense has trouble accepting this conviction or conclusion; in order for someone to be a victim someone else has to be the tyrant, tormentor, devil. If everyone is exclusively a victim, then no one is a victim.

Why is it that not a single group is ready to see itself as, at one time or another, both the side that produced victims and was a victim, too—which is probably closest to the truth. What is the attraction of the status of victim, since everyone clearly wants to be a victim? Why are people much readier to pity themselves as victims—which means losers, sufferers—than to be proud of the strength and skill of "their" people, who did not allow themselves to become victims or turned other people into victims? What need is satisfied when members of large groups such as ethnonationalities perceive themselves as victims and present themselves to others as being more suited to bear the title of victim than anyone else?

If you are the victim, you are the only one or the first one to be offered assistance by those who feel obliged to help the weaker—those who fared badly in the conflict, had the most casualties. It is easier for the powerful, at least in public, to justify assistance to weak, vulnerable victims than assistance to those believed to have produced the victims. The very fact that states' relations are not determined by moral principles, or are not the primary consideration, makes every state, particularly a large and powerful state, anxious to present itself as being more ethical than it really is.

Furthermore, being a victim means having the moral and material right to reprisal. There will be greater surprise if the victim forgives than if he or she exacts revenge. Everyone seems to expect the victim to settle accounts sooner or later, to return tit for tat, and to punish those who have made them a victim. If you are not a victim, your open or clandestine preparations for new warfare will be viewed with much less understanding. As a non-victim, you do not have the right to start a new round of bloodshed; you actually have no reason to do so, at least not an obvious one. If you are a victim, most people will know or suspect why you have taken up arms and will not be surprised at your belligerence.

That is why it is better to be a victim than a winner. If any ethnonational group wants to go to war again—tomorrow, in several years or centuries—it should not renounce the status of victim; moreover, it should carefully foster that status, constantly reminding itself and others. In addition, the victim always has a stronger motive to inflict the greatest harm, to destroy the other side or sides. In every conflict, the victim has a moral and psychological advantage over those who did not want, or did not know how, to create and/or preserve the image of themselves as victims. In a word, it is easier and more fitting to wage war if you are a victim than if you aren't.

The victim can never and dares not liberate himself/herself from the past; yet he or she counts on the future and even serves it. The victim is a prisoner of the past, and does everything for the sake of the future. The oppressor is satisfied, at least for a while, with plunder, defeat of the other side, and the harm that has been inflicted. In many cases, this lasts for a shorter time than the victim is prepared to view himself/herself primarily, or exclusively, as a victim.

Being a victim means having a long memory, sometimes several centuries long. Since, as a rule, memories of defeat last longer than memories of victory in both the individual and collective consciousness, the status of victim has a long life. It even outlives the defeat that the victim, in the meantime, has inflicted against those who in the past turned him into a victim.

The victim always gets off easy. He or she is more easily forgiven for breaching agreements, for not acknowledging the obvious, for stealing from or cheating those who extend a helping hand, for acting spitefully toward the oppressors, who keep repeating that they themselves have also been victims. The victim is expected to take advantage of his/her victimization as long and as often as possible, using it to justify every action, particularly those beneficial to him/her and detrimental to the other side. The victim is deeply surprised and even offended if anyone questions his/her right to do something, even if it is obviously wrong. The victim has rights that others do not have.

One of the particular advantages of being a victim is that the victim is considered by himself/herself and others as not responsible for his or her unfortunate fate. It is as though he or she became the victim through no fault of his/her own. The role of victim in the sequence of events that has led to becoming a victim is usually underestimated, not considered worthy of special attention, which certainly suits the victim. It is enough punishment that he or she is a victim; there is no need to examine whether and how much he or she might have contributed to this quite unenviable position. However, such an analysis would help to show that the roles of victim and oppressor are not clear-cut; rather, they intertwine, overlap, each side appearing in the role of the oppressor at times and in the role of the oppressed at others. Taken all together, this would destroy the established pattern of relations and be detrimental to the greater victim while helping the smaller victim.

As long as the victim is a victim, the other side is the wrongdoer, worthy of every condemnation and a most suitable target of ill will and negative emotions. The oppressor who has made me a victim will always be guilty of the fact that something is wrong with me, that I am unsuccessful, incompetent, not very wise, politically shortsighted, that "my" people are bickering, inclined to all kinds of foul dealings, and not really very enlightened. The oppressor who is to blame for my being a victim will be to blame when I am caught stealing, when it is shown that I am not the way I would like others to see me, and when it turns out that, ultimately, I am most similar to the one who has made me a victim.

If I am a victim I cannot be critical of myself, but I can be overly critical of those whom I believe to be the basic reason for my not having a very realistic view of events and relationships. Being a victim means being less critical since a victim, it is believed, is so humiliated, offended, and preoccupied with himself/herself that he or she is not able, even briefly, to forget that he or she is a victim. The victim acts and reacts with his or her emotions.

Listening as I have to people from different ethnonational groups in what was Yugoslavia, and thinking about the possible reasons—only some of which I have mentioned—for each one's conviction that they and their people are the sole and exclusive victims, I have come to the conclusion that the basic prerequisite for any sort of peace among ethnonational groups that fate and history have destined to live next to each other, is for them to stop considering themselves victims. I am not speaking of forgiving and forgetting but of the need for each side to start getting used to the fact that it is not just a victim. Surely no other role provides such powerful and abundant reasons for individuals and communities to become highly alienated from one another and consider the next conflict inevitable and thus all the more necessary. Ultimately, it is easy to be a victim; each person can find enough reasons in the present and past to consider himself/herself a victim. It is hard not to be a victim.

His Father Saved Him

D. is an old friend of my wife's. They worked in the same department at Sarajevo University and cooperated closely on numerous projects. Sometimes, usually after work, D. would come to our house, so I got to know him personally. He was extremely hardworking, completely devoted to his work, and showed no interest in social happenings—particularly not in politics. If D. were ever drawn into a conversation on a topic outside his profession, he had the habit of presenting his opinion, usually in a highly uncomplicated form, with the words "I, as a simple engineer..." It seemed as if he wanted to suggest his incompetence regarding matters from the broader social context, and to say that one should not ascribe very much importance to his words.

From D.'s brief comments on various events, it was not hard to conclude that he was very critical of the ruling regime and the state of society. Although a number of his critical remarks were well founded, it seemed to me that when he spoke of the social situation he threw out the baby with the bath water. He would usually dispute the very possibility of correcting mistakes, making the system more efficient, and bringing the government's declarations at least somewhat in line with reality. Surmising from his views and attitude towards current social happenings that D. felt somewhat excluded from society, I could not grasp what it was that stood in the way of his feeling otherwise: his nature, bad experience with some previous involvement outside the framework of his profession, or his deep-seated resistance to the political system such as it was.

D., as most academics, never drew attention to his ethnonational affiliation. He never tried to let others know or remind them that he was a Croat. One event, one anecdote, provides a good illustration of how little importance was given at the time to ethnonational affiliation among the academics. A rather large group of people was discussing who might be the next secretary of the party organization (at the university). According to the firmly established and strictly followed system, since the previous two secretaries were a Serb and a Muslim, respectively, the next party secretary was to be a Croat. D. turned to my wife with the proposal that she be nominated for the position. He was surprised when she told him that she did not fulfill the prerequisite, since she was not a Croat. Then someone suggested D. as the next secretary. My wife was even more surprised than D. had been a moment before. She assumed D. was a Serb. His first and last name made this entirely possible.

When D. applied for a teaching position at the university, my wife told me, a rumor reached the members of the selection committee that they should think twice before recommending D. as a teacher since his father had been a Ustasha. This rumor, it soon turned out, had been spread by a man who felt threatened by D.'s professional competence.

D. was quite upset by the rumors being spread about his father. It was as if the person who had started them and those who were spreading them had touched a very painful spot in his past. Not long after the story that D.'s father had been "on the other side" started to pass from one academic to another, D., in a rather gloomy mood, told my wife what had happened with his father and all his family.

D. was born in 1940. Near the end of World War II, his father was conscripted into the Domobrani (the Domobrani, meaning Home Guard, were created by the Ustasha government under Ante Pavelich soon after the proclamation of the so-called Independent State of Croatia in April 1941). As soon as the war was over he left for Argentina along with many others who were afraid that the new regime would persecute them. A year or two later he notified his family that he had bought tickets for them to come and join him and settle permanently in Argentina. D.'s mother was overjoyed at this. However, when she was about to leave with her two children, D.'s uncle—his father's brother, who was a highly ranked officer in the newly formed Yugoslav army—fiercely opposed their departure. He told D.'s mother that he had informed his brother that he was free to return to his homeland; there was no need to fear anyone or anything since he had committed no crime and would certainly not suffer any consequences for the fact that he had been with the Quisling forces for a short period of time.

The result of the uncle's intervention was that D., his mother, and his sister, who was four years younger, did not go to Argentina, but neither did their father return to Yugoslavia. In addition, all contact was broken between D.'s father and his family, and between D.'s uncle and D.'s mother and her children. D.'s father did not get in touch with them or reply to their letters. D.'s uncle, who lived in Belgrade, showed no desire even to see his brother's family, let alone help them in any way. It was as if they were to blame for the fact that D.'s father had not come back. D.'s mother, convinced that her brother-in-law was to blame for the fact that she was left with two small children and no husband, avoided even mentioning her brother-in-law's name. She tried to forget his very existence just as, over time, she became accustomed to the fact that her husband, although he might still be alive in the far-off world, no longer existed for her; he was dead for all practical purposes.

D. has dark memories from childhood. Shortages of all kinds are not what he remembers as being the worst. He suffered more than anything because he was branded as the child of a father who must have greatly sinned against his people since he could not come home. The scene when D.'s family was evicted from their apartment is etched very powerfully in his memory. One of the local power holders at the time had taken a fancy to their apartment and that, together with their label as the family of an enemy of the people who had fled the country—a label which seemed to stick for good—was enough of an explanation as to why they should be out in the street. D. distinctly remembers the moment of their eviction as a six-year-old child, holding tightly onto his little bicycle, which had been repaired many times, saying they had no right to take it away from him.

Later, when he grew up and started to earn quite a good living for the circumstances at the time, D. was extremely devoted to his immediate family and generously helped his mother and sister. D. never could and never wanted to forgive his father for breaking contact with this family, for completely ignoring his obligations as a husband and father—in short, for having forgotten them. He felt that his father could have and should have protected them against the great misfortunes they experienced through no fault of their own.

In D.'s eyes, his father was an example of what a father should not be, an example of a bad father. So he endeavored to be the exact opposite of his father, to be a more than good father. He seemed to be trying to show how different he was from his father's image, which he barely remembered, and prove to himself how much better he was than his father, how little he and his father had in common. Everything his father had failed to accomplish, he had to do. In so doing, he felt he would blacken his father's reputation even more, and make it clearer than ever how much less of a father his father had been.

At the end of the 1980s, several years before Yugoslavia's disintegration, D.'s uncle got in touch and invited D., his mother, and his sister to Belgrade. He was seriously ill and expected to die any moment. He had no children. He expressed his remorse, although not very openly, for the way he acted towards them over the long years, and even for impeding their departure for Argentina. He said he wanted to leave them a good share of his fortune. D., his mother, and sister refused the offer. They felt that he owed them too much for them to be able to forgive him.

Then came the war in Bosnia. D. stayed in Sarajevo until the end of 1994, working at jobs in his field, and helping the Bosnian government. The way he put it, the longer the war lasted the less welcome he felt in Sarajevo, particularly at work. So he decided to leave Sarajevo. He succeeded, with great difficulty, and soon opened his own firm in Zagreb.

When I met D. in Zagreb in the summer of 1998, he seemed satisfied. During our short conversation he told me that now he felt one thousand times more a Croat than the other Croats. Preoccupied by the shopping I had to do before leaving for the airport, I did not pay special attention to the words about how much of a Croat he felt. I simply registered them as being a bit strange—particularly for D.

At the very end of 2000, D. came to Sydney to visit his daughter. Then I had a chance to have a long talk with him. Among other things, he told me what had happened to him in the summer of 1995 as he was returning to Zagreb from his house on the coast with his daughter. He was taking the shortest route through the Knin Krajina area, where the Croatian army was making final preparations for, as they called it, the liberation of those areas from the Serbs. A Croatian soldier stopped him at one of the control points and asked for his identity card. D.'s first and last name aroused the soldier's considerable suspicion. His face turned dark and he looked inquisitively at D., who was overcome with fear. He was filled with the not-so-distant memories of unpleasant moments when he had been questioned at control points in Sarajevo, and later at many places as he crossed Bosnia, when he had been paralyzed by the uncertain outcome of his confirmation. He thought he had left behind him once and for all the fear that someone would find him suspicious because of his name or fear when a man approached him with a rifle in his hands, intent on checking and establishing whether D. was qualified to continue his trip—and even quite often whether he was worthy of continuing to live.

When D. received Croatian citizenship soon after his arrival in Zagreb he felt safe once again, even tranquil, just as he used to feel before the war. He thought he would never again have to feel humiliated and wretched just because his nationality was different from the person whose rifle was pointed at him. But now a soldier from his new state, a Croat just like him, had started things all over again. It was as if the soldier wanted to show D. how premature it was to believe that being the same ethnonationality as the man in uniform meant you were safe. Or maybe D. had fallen into a trap? Maybe the soldier who was looking at him suspiciously wasn't a Croat at all? Maybe he was just hiding behind the uniform of a Croatian soldier. The area was not far from the position held by the Serbs. D. was completely confused, terrified. Pressured by fear, he searched as hard as he could for an answer to the puzzling situation, which was growing more tense by the moment and thus dangerous for him, but he could find no solution—nothing that would save him and his child.

Finally, the soldier asked him what his father's name was. When D. answered that his father's name was Rudolf, the scowl left the soldier's face; as though relieved. (The name Rudolf is quite common among the Croats. It does not exist among the Serbs and the Muslims.) He indicated to D. to continue on his way, warning him that it would have been smarter to take another route.

This incident seemed to be a turning point in D.'s attitude toward his father and toward his new homeland, Croatia. The very mention of his father's name had freed him from the nightmare of humiliation and uncertainty. He had once been ashamed of his father, suffered because of him, condemned his father a thousand times; he hadn't wanted to know anything about him. Now, all of a sudden, his father had become his savior—someone who, although long dead, had opened the way, provided him safe passage, protected him when danger loomed overhead. The bad father had become a good father, a guardian father. During the conversation, D. spoke to me about his life in Croatia and repeated several times that he had a great pedigree. Those were his exact words, "I have a great pedigree."

This is not the end of the story. D., who had once been extremely uninterested in political events, became an enthusiastic supporter of Franjo Tudjman and his policies. He boasted that he had read all of Tudjman's works, emphasizing that in terms of Europe perhaps only Churchill was his equal. Thus, he was greatly saddened by the HDZ (Croatian Democratic Community) loss at the last elections, and considered Tudjman's death an irredeemable loss for the Croatian people.

I don't know whether D. ever forgave his father for forgetting his wife and children, for turning his back on them when they needed him most. One thing was more than obvious, though; after several decades D. and his father were reconciled.

The Individual and the
Collective in Ethnonationalism

When listening to an ethnonationalist ardently defend his/her views and beliefs and, of course, greatly exaggerate in all respects either by aggrandizing his/her own side or belittling other sides, one of the many questions that arises is: Why is he or she talking like that? Is it at his/her own initiative because his/her personality dictates, or is he or she expressing ethnonationalistic views under the influence of specific external circumstances?

With such questions, the old dilemma of nature or nurture arises, as it almost always does whenever we want to establish which is more decisive in determining someone's characteristics: individual preferences or dislikes or the influence of environment. The dilemma is artificial, of course, because a person is exposed to external influences from birth. These external influences become an integral part of the individual to the extent that not a single living being, develops completely protected, from the influence of his/her environment. Even what seems to come "straight from nature," what a person brings with her/him into the world, has already been influenced by the environment in the form of the pregnant woman's nourishment, any disease she might have had during pregnancy, her psychic state during pregnancy, the conditions during the baby's delivery, and so on.

This is why I consider it fitting to formulate the above dilemma in the following way: How much influence do individual psychological factors, on the one hand, and social (economic, political, etc.) factors, on the other, have on the adoption of ethnonationalistic views and beliefs? In other words, how much does being an ethnonationalist depend on the kind of personality an individual has, and how much on the conditions in which he or she lives, who his/her friends are, which politicians he or she believes, his/her personal experiences with members of other ethnonational groups, and so on.

The very fact that epidemic nationalism—that is, ethnonationalism that has spread to a large part or the greater part of an (ethno)national group—is so prevalent indicates that individual differences are not crucial to the onset of ethnonationalism. It might be better to speak of the general inclination all people have, without exception, towards ethnonationalism, or more precisely towards the ethnonationalism-like behavioral pattern. This inclination, historically, appears first in the form of parochialism, then as tribalism, then ethnonationalism, and so on. In this regard, George Orwell accurately noted, "The nationalist's loves and hatreds . . . are a part of the makeup of most of us, whether we like it or not" (1945: 346).

It is impossible to explain the rapid expansion of ethnonationalistic passions and views in ethnic times without this general psychological-anthropological inclination towards the ethnonationalism-like behavioral pattern. It can be considered one of the basic conditions for engendering a specific type of behavior, manner of thinking, and feeling that in the right historical circumstances takes on the features of ethnonationalism.

It seems that what might be called group mentality in the broad sense forms this psychological-anthropological basis on which parochialism, ethnocentrism, tribalism, and ethnonationalism grow, while maintaining all the differences between these phenomena. Their basic common denominator in the psychological sense is the *we-they* syndrome, characterized by partiality, friendly feelings, an uncritical attitude towards those who belong to the same group, and excessive criticism, animosity, and even open hostility towards those who do not belong to our group; the assumption of *us against them*, insisting on a clear demarcation between us and those who are not one of us and the readiness to sacrifice ourselves to preserve what is *ours from them* or what is *theirs*. Group conflict is eternal. All that changes is the type of group. In this sense, Hans Magnus Enzensberger correctly remarked, "Sectional self-interest and xenophobia are anthropological constants which predate every rationalization. Their universal distribution indicates that they are older than all known societies" (1994:106).

The crux of the matter is people's psychologically-anthropologically based readiness to act and react in accordance with the dictates of the principle "amity inside-enmity outside." External circumstances to a greater extent and individual personal characteristics to a lesser extent will induce people to put this potential into effect and start exhibiting the syndrome's symptoms more or less explicitly and consistently.

The stamp of ethnonationalism is given by the myths, collective memories, value system, and traditions that are specific to each (ethno)national group, in addition to suitable external conditions, the individual's special personal inclination towards the ethnonationalism of a similar behavior pattern, and group mentality which, we have seen, is universal to man. There is no ethnonationalism without a collective name, a myth about common ancestors and the ethnonational group's past golden age, as well as a common language and pretensions to a specific (sacred) territory that belongs exclusively to the ethnonational group. Finally, every ethnonational group considers the preservation of its cultural identity to be the only true guarantee of its survival. All this forms the ethnosymbolic, to use a term of Anthony D. Smith (1986:190–198).

Returning to the title of this essay, I am compelled to answer the question of whether there are individuals who are more inclined to accept ethnonationalism, who react more readily to the provocation of ethnonationalism (or parochialism, tribalism, etc.). The answer is affirmative only if ethnonationalism is looked upon not as a unique phenomenon without historical parallels but as a historically specific form of behavioral pattern. This behavioral pattern, in addition to the *we-they* syndrome and others, is characterized by: anti-individualism; advocating the greatest uniformity in the views and feelings of the community members; intolerance; degradation of what is rational; greater susceptibility to emotional stimuli; extremism; the simplification of complex relationships; freedom from individual responsibility, which is transferred to the collective; rigidity; propensity for conformism or subjugation to authority; aggressive feelings towards those who are considered inferior.

There is no specific set of individual characteristics and propensities that includes all the psychological characteristics encountered by ethnonationalists. In other words, there is no specific type of personality that in non-ethnonationalistic (non-ethnic) times exhibits *all* the feelings and behavioral and ideological characteristics of the ethnonationalists. In the same vein, based on the psychological makeup of a specific individual, it is impossible to say whether, in given historical, social and political circumstances, he or she will certainly or almost certainly become an ethnonationalist. There are, however, personality types that have specific psychological traits and tendencies characteristic of ethnonationalists. It can be said that such individuals are more inclined to adopt ethnonationalism than

individuals without such individual-psychological characteristics, who comprise the far greater part of the general
population.

What are these personality types? Whenever a specific
form of behavior, thought, and feeling becomes socially preferred as being essential for the group's survival, people are
exposed to social-psychological pressure to accept this behavioral pattern. The greater the number of people who behave
in accordance with this pattern, the greater the collective's
pressure on the individual to conform.

It should not be forgotten that different social-psychological processes play a very important role in the expansion of
ethnonationalism and its collectivization. Ethnonationalism
as both an individual and group phenomenon, in both its endemic and epidemic forms, is never self-created. No one becomes and remains an ethnonationalist for the sole reason
that it satisfies a personal need that has arisen indepen-
dently of how others in the same family, community, political
party, or same area act and feel.

People are more inclined to conformism if they feel basically insecure and vulnerable, lack confidence in their own
abilities, need to have someone else direct and control their
lives, have no spontaneous emotions, and are inhibited.
When ethnonationalism starts to spread in the community
and becomes standard social behavior, those who tend to respond quickly to social pressure include individuals with an
external, rather than internal, locus of control, individuals
who believe they have only one option instead of several regarding how to behave, think, and feel in various situations;
and individuals who are *high self-monitors* (M. Snyder,
1987).

Among all personality types, the *authoritarian* has attracted the greatest attention of scholars. It is said to predis-
pose the individual to act ethnonationalistically in suitable
socioeconomic and political circumstances. The relationship
between the authoritarian personality and the ethnona-

tionalistic behavioral pattern can therefore be used to analyze the participation of the individual–personal and the social (collective) in ethnonationalism.

In the years after World War II, a group of social scientists
in America, led by Theodor Adorno (1950), was given the task
of identifying which personality type, if it existed at all, was
inclined to behave, believe, and feel like the promoters of national socialism in Germany. After several years of research,
they established that such a personality exists and they
called it the *authoritarian personality*.

What are the basic characteristics of the authoritarian
personality? The authoritarian personality tends to be con-
ventional and insists on respect for the dominant group standard. Since he or she does not have internal criteria and
views, the authoritarian individual must accept and respect
conventions. Without external support (the authority of some
person or public opinion), the authoritarian is unable to say
what is right and what is not, requiring conventions as a basic guideline. This is also why he or she wants to submit to a
leader (authoritarian submissiveness). Authoritarian aggressiveness is closely connected to authoritarian submissiveness. Aggressiveness is directed towards those who are
considered inferior, as a rule—those outside the group.

The authoritarian personality is also rigid in emotional and
cognitive respects. Rigidity, narrowing one's field of interest
and critical awareness, is connected to two other propensities
of the authoritarian personality: the tendency towards bias
and stereotypes. Rigidity and a propensity towards stereotypes do not allow the authoritarian personality to have any
doubts, let alone an understanding of nuances and views and
evaluations that are found in the broad area between black
and white. This is why the authoritarian personality cannot
avoid falsifying reality with its diversity of shapes and multitude of passages between two or more extremes.

If we bear in mind the characteristics of ethnonational
mentality, that is, the basic principles of nationalistic ideol-

ogy, it is not hard to note similarities between the authoritarian personality and the ethnonationalist. The authoritarian personality rejects and despises those he or she considers weak, dishonest, and immoral. The nationalist feels similarly about members of the rival ethnonational group. Both the authoritarian personality and the ethnonationalist are rigid, inclined to self-aggrandizement, moralism, conventionalism, dichotomization, bias, and stereotypes. Neither can stand dilemmas; they like an unambiguous, black-and-white world. In addition, Adorno and his associates identified authoritarian personalities as being readier than others to respond to antidemocratic and anti-Semitic propaganda. Do authoritarian personalities react more readily and rapidly to nationalistic propaganda, too?

Every consideration of the relationship between the authoritarian personality and nationalism inevitably raises much broader questions regarding the relationship between personality and the environment. This relationship is given a different interpretation within different concepts and theories. For example, endeavoring to conceptualize the relationship among society, social structures, and the individual, Erich Fromm (1947) introduced the category of *social character*, something shared more or less by all people in a specific community. Social character contains internalized social demands and is thus the mediator between the individual and society, ensuring the duration of the specific social relationship.

Returning to the question of the relationship between the authoritarian personality (syndrome, character) and the social environment, it seems to me that it has several forms.

First, the dynamics of family relationships form the authoritarian character of the child and later adult. Such a personality corresponds to the authoritarian individual described by Adorno and associates. He or she has the potential to accept and develop fascist views, since he or she is readier than other people to respond to antidemocratic, primarily ethnocentric stimuli (i.e., propaganda), both when a distinct authority is sending the message and when he or she is in stressful social surroundings.

Second, authoritarian behavior represents the norm (standard) in some social environments, and people behave like authoritarian personalities not under the pressure of internal needs but so they don't stand out from people around them. Living in an environment in which authoritarian behavior is the norm, people become accustomed to the authoritarian behavior pattern and adopt it completely.

Third, the authoritarian behavior pattern is the form by which a specific group or social layer, members of a specific social class, adjust to the social atmosphere; to be more precise, the authoritarian pattern responds to their special position in the social structure.

Fourth, a number of people feel incompetent, uncertain, unable to find self-reliance because of influencing factors and circumstances, both emotional—cognitive and upbringing—as well as educational. Such people see authoritarian behavior as a way to overcome these unpleasant feelings or at least fight them more successfully. These people can spontaneously develop authoritarian behavior, because they very readily and quickly react to every social promotion ("offer") of the authoritarian behavior model.

Fifth, current social, economic, and political events in an environment can generate similar feelings in one person or most of the community members—that is, feelings of insecurity, disorientation, vulnerability, incompetence, less value. Such feelings appear in people, for example, when large normative systems disintegrate, when state communities fall apart, or when the economic situation drastically worsens and the living standard of most people suddenly drops sharply.

The authoritarian pattern, owing to its inherent characteristics, can appear as a reaction and attempt to free oneself from such unpleasant feelings. On the whole, the authoritarian pattern is potentially a common form of reaction, a common denominator of man's various attempts to oppose and cope with the subjectively very unpleasant feelings of uncertainty, threat, tension, incompetence, and lesser value, regardless of the origin of these feelings.

We have seen that, in terms of appearance, the authoritarian and nationalistic patterns have much in common. Nationalistic views and beliefs can and often do serve the same function as the authoritarian behavior pattern. This reflects the link between nationalism and the authoritarian personality, and the broader relationship between the individual and the collective in ethnonationalism.

Finally, the difference between social behavior caused by the need to conform to the social norm and that which is dictated primarily by needs resulting from personality structure lies not only in their origin but also in how much and how easily they change. Needs arising from the structure of the individual's psychological makeup are more difficult to change. On the other hand, social views and behavior that result from group pressure and/or express the need to conform to the prevailing social norm, change with a change in the circumstances that produced them.

The relationship between the individual and the collective in ethnonationalism is circular, not linear. In addition, a generalized consideration of this relationship does not have to be a good guide to determining why a person became an ethnonationalist. We can only draw near to answering the question of the relationship between the individual and the collective in ethnonationalism by analyzing each individual case in which ethnonationalistic views and beliefs are exhibited. There is a unique, specific, share of the personal and collective in each individual appearance of ethnonationalism.

WORKS CITED

Adorno, T.W.; Frenkel-Brunswik, E.; Levinson, D.J.; and Sanford, R.N. *The authoritarian personality*. New York: Norton, 1950.

Enzensberger, H.M. *Civil wars: From L.A. to Bosnia.* New York: The New Press, 1994.

Fromm, E. *Man for himself.* New York: Rinehart, 1947.

Orwell, G. "Notes on nationalism," in S. Orwell and S. Angus (eds.), *Collected essays: Journalism and letters of George Orwell,* vol. 3. New York: Harcourt Brace Jovanovich, 1945.

Smith, D.S. *Nationalism and modernity.* London, New York: Routledge, 1998.

Snyder, M. *Private appearances/Private realities.* New York: Freeman, 1987.

A Good Enough Enemy

There is no war until brother strikes out against brother. Two people never feel greater animosity for each other than when they resemble each other. This can also be said about feelings of intimacy and love; they are the strongest between kindred souls, between people who have much more that connects them than separates them. In other words, we can never feel such powerful hatred or love for someone with very different affinities, characteristics, origins, and so on, as we can for someone who reminds us of ourselves. Can this general condition of attracting and repelling among individuals be applied to peoples, to entire collectives, to ethnonational groups? Is it true that members of related peoples are most inclined to fall into one another's arms as well as go for the jugular?

With due respect for the magnitude of the differences between individual and collective psychology, it seems to me that individuals and collectives, and even entire peoples, act in a similar manner towards those who resemble them. Since the times in which we live have resulted, for many reasons, in people's attention being riveted more on hatred than on love, I will focus on two possible reasons for the disproportionately large animosity among peoples whose similarity at first glance would justify their peaceful coexistence more than their mutual aversion—in the milder variation—and mutual bloodletting, in the more vehement variation.

There are many reasons why one ethnic group might have numerous characteristics (habits, customs, views, and affinities) that are similar to those of another ethnic group. Perhaps both were or still are part of a larger cultural group; both peoples suffered or are still suffering under the rule of the same conqueror from whom, willingly or not, they acquired many common characteristics; one of the peoples held the other under subjugation for too long a time, with the same consequences as when both were under the rule of a common enemy; two peoples have been living right next to each other for centuries and thus took from each other not only goods but also habits, affinities, views; fate and history have destined that two ethnic groups live within the same administrative-political entity, and so they have mixed together physically, mentally, and spiritually, sometimes until no distinctions separate them.

When it happens for one or more of the above reasons that two ethnic groups find each other similar, then they need each other for good times and bad. In both these cases differences between them, regardless of how small, are often overemphasized; the two groups thus turn out to be, and present themselves as being, quite distant in all respects, foreign, different, couldn't-be-more-different.

Every man, just like every group of people, must establish his individuality, which means his identity. Establishing our identity means showing ourselves and others how unique we are, how special and different we are from everyone else. It is only when identity has been established that the individual and the collective feel certain of their existence. Clearly visible borders between individualities or ethnonational beings help them to survive in times that directly or indirectly threaten their singularity, if not their very existence.

Identity is more obvious and recognizable, not to say greater, the more it differs from the image of other persons or other peoples. Naturally, there is no need for an ethnic group to take pains to show how different it is from those who resemble it very little or not at all—either physically or in dress, beliefs, language, or favorite food. But it takes great skill and effort to distinguish oneself from those who resemble you. This is usually done in three ways: by hushing up or loudly denying every similarity between me and you, between my people and your people, particularly those similarities that are more than obvious; by producing, which means inventing, differences; and finally, by overemphasizing actually existing differences, so that they become an absolute obstacle to mutual understanding and closeness. Once huge differences have thus been established where there actually are none, the next step is slow and almost inescapable. Those who were close and are now distant become infinitely alienated, thereby confirming and ensuring the extent of the differences between "them" and "us," and the strength and steadfastness of each one's identity. Hatred towards similar ethnic groups is the price that some ethnic groups pay either to establish and/or ensure their own identity.

The other way in which the similar traits of two ethnic groups become the basis for animosity between them is somewhat more complex. Except when they are depressed, people rarely speak ill of themselves, because they never think of themselves as bad in any way. People simply can't stand it when they have unpleasant feelings or aggressive and destructive impulses; they shrink from their bad qualities. They do not want such negative emotions to be a part of their personality.

So what should they do with them? How can they get the upper hand? They project them onto other people, onto other ethnic groups who thereby become evil, unprincipled, genocidal, malicious, etc. Then they exceedingly detest and hate their own bad traits—in other people. The fact that others are bad is a sufficient and necessary reason for us to hate them even more.

An ideal object upon which to project our bad selves is not someone whose characteristics are quite different from ours, with whom we have little or almost nothing in common, someone foreign to us. In other words, since we are projecting our own "dirty" feelings, negative notions, fears and impulses, the one on whom we project our "bad selves"—and this happens on the unconscious level—should be someone similar to us, close to us, just like us, and yet different from us. After someone who has many characteristics in common with us has thus, owing to some sort of mental defense mechanism, become the bearer of "our bad selves," we must constantly be on guard to keep our distance from him (i.e., "our bad selves"), convincing ourselves and others of these huge and insurmountable differences that exist between us, our ethnic group, and the other ethnic group.

This phenomenon is the source of what is called the *narcissism of small differences*. When we have projected what we do not like in ourselves onto others, then we simply have to maintain the firmest possible distance between the "enemy" and us. This distance serves as some sort of shield that prevents our undesirable parts, impulses, everything that is bad in "our people" from returning to our collective ego. For this reason, regardless of how small the real differences may be they play a great psychological role. The enemy must be close enough to us so we can project our "bad selves" onto him, and far enough away and odious enough, so that our own evil does not endanger us. To put it succinctly, the enemy must be a good enough enemy (H. Stein, 1987).

This, however, is not the end of the story. By turning another ethnic group into the enemy we put ourselves in a dependent position. We become prisoners of the enemy we have created, who we almost cannot do without. This reduces our adaptability; many alternatives become inaccessible that might help us be our own selves, custodians of our own identity, powerful enough to create room within ourselves for "our bad selves," and face the fact that we ourselves are bad, too. Only an ethnic group that is able to establish and safeguard its identity using means other than solely or primarily emphasizing their uniqueness (with the attendant conviction that no one can understand them) is able to live with other ethnic groups without being on more or less constant bad terms with them. They will be greatly assisted in this regard by the readiness to accept their share of the evil without projecting it onto another ethnic group with whom they have a great deal in common.

It is some sort of paradox and irony. A strategy of self-defense intended to establish and strengthen our identity, the identity of our people, and the nice feeling that we are only well-intentioned, honest and good, can, unwillingly, contribute to our self-destruction. And that is exactly what happens, more often than we might think.

WORK CITED

Stein, H. *Developmental time, cultural space*. Norman: University of Oklahoma Press, 1987.

The Boomerang of
Impassioned Bias

Radio and television broadcasts in Sarajevo and its vicinity can be heard and seen from both the Muslim and Serbian sides. They report on primarily the same events, although as a rule the same event is shown and interpreted quite differently by these two warring parties.

As circumstances would have it, in the late summer of 1992 I was on both one side and the other, among the civilians and soldiers of both warring parties. Each side told me that the media on the other side were extremely non-objective, biased, rooted for only one side, and were disrespectful of the truth.

Those who were more critical, or rather less uncritical, and able to observe this mess with some distance were of the opinion that perhaps it was natural for there to be two truths. There was a war on, they said, and propaganda is a component part of war. Apparently even before the war there had been several truths about events in this area, although no one talked about them—at least not out loud. So one should not have been surprised that several truths existed during warfare, in a heightened, belligerent form. There were as many truths as warring parties.

Those on both sides who were less critical, thus more impassioned, accepted at face value everything offered by their media, and placed unlimited trust in almost every statement or comment that was seen or heard on their side's television and radio. As far as I could tell, the number of these media "oppressed" and "believers" was remarkably higher than the number who had not fallen prey to only one truth. It was interesting to note that many of them, defending their views in a way or perhaps showing their openmindedness, said that their "information" and convictions were not drawn from only one side; they almost regularly listened to and watched the radio and TV messages of the other side. Therefore, their views and opinions were the result of free choice; they opted for the media source that, in their opinion, did not twist facts and circumvent the truth.

Continuing the conversation—and this is actually what led me to write these lines—these "less critical" observers would say that, in the long run, they really weren't interested in what the other side had to say about itself which was, of course all positive, all the best—as if they were miserable, imperiled, innocent, righteous, truthful, had been attacked for no reason, were only defending their homes, and so on. But, they emphasized, they could not forgive the other side for speaking so badly about their side. I had the impression that they actually wanted to say the following: "Let them say whatever they want about themselves. We know perfectly well what they're like; no one has to tell us about them, they least of all. But we are sincerely hurt by the fact that their news programs disgrace and slander us, insult and disparage us so much." And then they would usually add: "The fact that the other side is spreading such boldfaced lies about us gives us additional strength and more than enough reason to destroy them." It was as if these lies about them that the other side was spreading gave them additional (or enough) reason to intensify their attacks against those who produced them. In their eyes, the lies gave them one more powerful argument to persevere in carrying out their original intention, regardless of the cost: Destroy the enemy, the more the better, and if possible annihilate him. It seems to me that what the other side said about them provided additional impetus for even greater ill will, hatred, and aggressiveness, both towards the individuals spreading the lies and, even more, towards all those on the other side. Their reasoning was that, "Those people on the other side certainly knew that our side is far from being so sinister. Yet those people aren't saying a word against their media. Quite the contrary, they agree with them, acknowledge they are right, put their complete trust in them."

In essence, they said that when the other side thinks and speaks so poorly of them, when they ascribe to their side actions they have never committed, impute to them ideas and aspirations things that never crossed their minds, when they demonize them beyond all measure, this only goes to show that the other side is incorrigibly, to put it mildly, malicious and incendiary. It is the source of so much evil that in order to save themselves they must annihilate the other side—for good, without mercy. I wonder if the producers and propagators of the "truth" in the war propaganda ever once thought that their activities might have such an effect, which is clearly undesirable for their side, for what they represent, and for the interests of those for whom they are working.

The easiest thing to do is paint the world black and white. There is practically no risk involved and not much ingenuity required. It sticks to an established stratagem: Our side is only and exclusively good; the others are only and exclusively bad. I suppose that behind this practice lies the conviction that painting the other side in the darkest colors will raise the fighting spirit of "our" side, "our" fighters. They will be given justification and reason for even fiercer attacks against the enemy, who is more wicked than the devil himself. However, what propagandizers forget is that such a media policy achieves the same, if not greater, effect on the opposite side: it increases hatred, aggressiveness, the desire to destroy and have a final showdown. Messages that disparage the other side and show those on "the other side of the barricade" in the worst possible light do not demoralize them; quite the contrary, these messages incite their anger and strengthen their determination to put an end to those who show them as being immoral, inhumane, and worthy of utter condemnation.

There is one other rather unexpected effect of the mass media's endless defamation of those in the opposite, rival group. If you tell someone for days and months that he or she is bad, immoral, genocidal, with no respect for the elderly and no concern for the young, he or she will—assuming, of course, that he or she is not like that—first get upset, protest, and then over time decide to identify with the image that others are persistently spreading about her/him. Psychologically, it is not easy to tolerate for any period of time the huge discrepancy between what we more or less objectively are and what others keep on saying about us, or how they portray us. People rather often find a way to end the resulting stress by behaving in accordance with the image of them that others have created. By taking over the role that others have forced on them, so to speak, they greatly assuage their dissatisfaction, anger, and the feeling of constantly being torn between *we are* and *we are not*.

The way it is now, the machinery of war propaganda is working to the detriment of both warring parties. The best way to understand just how much truth lies in this statement is to spend time with members of both sides in a conflict. During times of war, however, this requirement is usually hard to meet.

Endemic and Epidemic Ethnonationalists

When nationalistic beliefs inundate a society—which is what happened in almost all the areas of what until recently was the second Yugoslavia—people who were somehow able to avoid the floodtide, and those from distant regions, often wonder what relations were like among the people of different ethnic groups before the advent of ethno-nationalism. Was there anything in their relations that indicated so little time would be needed for the appearance of such great mutual hatred, hostility, and fratricide?

The question is too complex to allow a simple answer, since interethnic relations varied from one area to another in the second Yugoslavia during different periods of its existence. In addition, the nature of interethnic relations was influenced by an extremely large number of factors, some variable and some constant. To cite only some of them: the prevailing policy of interethnic relations; personal and/or family experience with members of other ethnonationalities, particularly during critical periods—earlier interethnic conflicts, periods of deprivation, serious social disturbances; living permanently or periodically in ethnonationally homogeneous or heterogeneous environments in which the prevailing attitude was traditionally of mutual cooperation or conflict with the population of a different ethnonational origin; life on the fringe or in the middle of larger ethnonational entities; the frequency of communication with people who had a primarily understanding attitude or emphatically biased view of interethnic relations; the degree of family ties with people from other ethnonationalities, and so on.

I lived in Sarajevo from just about the first to the last days of the second Yugoslavia. In terms of the relative number of members of the three largest ethnonational groups in one single urban entity, Sarajevo was unlike almost any other town in the second Yugoslavia. In the same vein (is it a coincidence?), in the recent war (1992–1995), Bosnia was unlike any other area of Yugoslavia in terms of the ferocity of the fighting between the three ethnonational communities. For this reason it might be interesting to look at a phenomenological typology of the relations that Sarajevo's inhabitants had with people from other ethnonationalities during the two or three decades before the outbreak of war.

(1) A number of people paid no attention to other people's ethnonationality. It might even be said that they didn't notice it. Ethnonational affiliation did not play any role in their choice of neighbors or friends, in bestowing their trust, and expressing their feelings towards friends and strangers. If for any reason they became aware of the ethnonationality of the people with whom they communicated more or less regularly, this did not arouse either positive or negative emotions. If circumstances were such that they spontaneously, or at someone's suggestion, made a connection between the characteristics and affinities of some person and their ethnonational origin, they did not have the least tendency to make

generalizations and conclude that all or most members of other ethnonational communities were identical in characteristics, habits, preferences, etc., or to believe that such characteristics of other ethnonational provenience were less worthy than those of their own ethnic group.

(2) A number of people, in one way or another, were conscious most of the time of the differences between themselves and the people of other ethnonationalities. When asked what those differences actually were, they were usually unable to describe them in any detail or, being unskilled at formulating their convictions or observations, they would resort to stereotypes such as the Serbs are belligerent, the Croats are cultured, and the Muslims take pains not to arouse anyone's anger. Those with more education explained differences among people of different ethnonationalities by the differences in the religion, history, culture, and so on, of the ethnonational groups.

Awareness of ethnonational differences was neither a reason nor a pretext for people in this group to behave in any special way towards "those others," to be suspicious of them, avoid them, or shy away from them. Convinced that "by the nature of things" people who bowed to Mecca, turned their eyes to Rome, and kissed the patriarch's hand could not be the same, they nonetheless left the possibility wide open that there were people from all three ethnonational groups whose characteristics were closer to either of the other two groups than to those with whom they share the same ethnonational origin.

(3) Those conscious of ethnonational differences also felt that there were indisputable differences between people from different ethnic groups; they very often linked the daily behavior and long-term preoccupations of the people around them with their ethnonationality, which was also used to explain such behavior. They expected it, and thus, normal, for people to bear in mind the ethnonational origin of the people with whom they came into contact and entered mutually binding relationships, particularly when making long-term

personal, family, business, etc., plans. They also believed that regardless of how much a person worked for the good of the whole country, which means people of different ethnonationalities, he must never neglect the interests of his own ethnonational group. They were patriots on the public political scene and devoted to the cultural-religious traditions of their ethnic group in their private and family life. They said it was only the intentional bowing to the obvious—that is, the need to curry favor with the daily political order—that was preventing people from using the real key to explain most of the conduct and strivings of the people around them, to grasp the hidden reason and meaning behind people's actions. Thus, for example, the lack of their own social advancement, which they believed to have been deserved long ago, was quite readily ascribed to the ethnona- tionality of the people who, in their specific case, made decisions about their merits. The same principle was used to explain the "real reason" for someone's social or professional achievements in cases where such success was not to their liking.

People in this group usually fostered beliefs about the close link between ethnonationality and religion, with religious affiliation often being considered the deciding factor that brought people together or separated them, turned people towards each other or against each other.

It should be noted that in most cases people with such views of the place and role of ethnonationality in people's relationships were not militantly against people from other ethnonationalities. They considered—in peaceful times— that one should simply bear in mind that differences were inevitable in the commitments and interests of people from different ethnonationalities; this was some sort of constant that could not be questioned. This awareness and conviction, however, did not hinder them from successfully collaborating with people from other ethnonationalities, socializing with them, and sharing laughter and sorrow with them.

(4) Finally, there were people who felt that the simple fact that someone was from another ethnonationality justified their hostile feelings towards them. They were expansive and quite imaginative when explaining to themselves and others the origin of such negative emotions towards people from another ethnonationality, ascribing to them solely bad characteristics. They were adamant in their conviction that "those others" had been like that since the beginning of time and thus there was no reason to believe they could ever change. They constantly expressed their fear of "those others" getting too close to them, convinced that "those others" were only interested in subjugating them and depriving them of their cultural uniqueness and religion. They were therefore obsessed with demarcations: the stricter, more comprehensive, and permanent the better. Although they rarely said that "keeping their gun sights aimed at those others" was the only acceptable attitude towards those who were not from "their" people, they most often acted in accordance with this principle. Every seemingly conciliatory move by the "opposite side" was interpreted as new proof of the shrewdness and hypocrisy of "those others." They never doubted for a moment that there would be new conflicts with "them"; the only uncertainty was when they would actually take place.

Aware of how much their convictions clashed with the ruling political doctrine, those with such views of people from other ethnonationalities did not openly express their opinions. They primarily discussed the grounds and justification for their views within the circle of like-minded thinkers, far from the eyes and ears of the public; or they expressed their opinions using the Aesopian language of different artistic creations. Those who were less skilled at hiding their ideas, those who were braver, and those who were fanatically devoted to the idea that, in essence, there was not and could not be peace among peoples of different ethnonationalities, came into conflict with the law and were sentenced. Marginalized in society or behind prison bars, they waited for time to prove that all those who did not share their views and beliefs had been wrong.

This brief review of the four basic types of relations among people who belonged to different ethnonationalities in the extremely heterogeneous ethnonational environment that was Bosnia as a whole, and particularly its capital, Sarajevo, should give the reader a better idea of what the situation was like. Sentimental, nostalgic memories of all the ethnic groups in prewar Sarajevo living in the greatest love, brotherhood, and unity are far from the truth.

The other question posed at the beginning of this text about whether anything in the relations among people of different ethnonationalities forewarned that they might turn against one another, so quickly, and to such a large extent, is another matter. If we direct our attention to those in the fourth and partially the third typologies presented, we might conclude that it is not surprising that conflicts arose between different ethnonational groups; what is surprising is that they did not arise even earlier. At this juncture in our discussion of the ethnonational heterogeneous context of prewar Sarajevo, let me make the following assertion (whose grounds could only be confirmed or rejected by empirical analysis—which, unfortunately, was never made). In Sarajevo in the decades preceding the war, members of the first and second groups were more numerous than members from the third and fourth groups.

It is at this point that many highly interesting questions crop up. What were the relations among the above four divisions of the population? Did they ignore one another openly or implicitly, did they cooperate with one another, or did they simply live next to one another, without bothering one another? Did the members of each group prefer to socialize with people from their same group? Did people from the fourth group and somewhat from the third prepare for the war, did they (only) initiate it, or was their role restricted to being the ones primarily counted on and abundantly relied upon by those who, as it is sometimes claimed, came from the outside and brought fratricide to Bosnia? During the war and now, in what has been called the postwar period, were members of the third and particularly the fourth group, the most active protagonists of ethnonationalism as an idea and in practice, as they so clearly were in the prewar period?

There is no doubt that members of the last two and particularly the fourth group from the above typology, were the core that maintained and spread the idea of ethnonationalism; this means that they were the core of the conflict that recently ended and will be the core of all future inter-ethnic conflicts in this area.

There is one thing, however, that should not be overlooked when discussing inter-ethnic conflicts anywhere, including in Bosnia and Sarajevo. Ethnonationalism only becomes truly relevant when it spreads to a larger or the largest part of the population in an environment. Therefore, the answer to conflicts inspired by ethnonationalism—where do they come from, why do they appear, and so on—lies not so much in the ethnonationalists who are endemic in a specific environment as in the larger part of the population that, until recently, was not inclined to ethnonationalistic views and convictions. In other words, when we try to find out why ethnonationalism flares up in public, why ethnonationalism becomes the only desirable social pattern of behavior, we should try to find the reasons and mechanisms whereby people from the first and second groups became avid, if not the most ardent, ethnona- tionalists. Without their transformation, regardless of how temporary or fleeting, ethnonationalism could not endanger the social order all that much. As paradoxical as it may sound, ethnonationalism as a mass movement can exist without people from the third and fourth groups, but certainly not without people from the first and second groups. Endemic nationalists are important for ethnonationalists, but their strength lies in epidemic ethnonationalism.

Inverse Ethnonationalism

It is well known that there are different types of ethnonationalism. I came to know one of the rare forms, which has yet to be described, through one of my best friends.

My wife and I have been close friends with Dijana and Dragan (names are not real) for years. In 1992, at the beginning of the war in Bosnia, Dragan was almost sixty and Dijana was three years younger. Dragan is a Serb and Dijana a Croat. This fact has never been of any consequence in our friendship but, as the reader will see, it proved to be very important in this story. Dragan's family comes from a small town in eastern Bosnia. His father had been an Orthodox priest and served for many years in an old Orthodox church in Sarajevo. Dijana's family is from the island of Korcula in Croatia. Dijana and Dragan met while studying sanitation engineering in Belgrade. After graduation they settled down in Sarajevo. They have no children.

Several years before the war, Dragan opened a private consulting firm involved in water management. He was very successful, and this soon resulted in a substantial rise in Dragan and Dijana's living standard and in Dragan's self-respect and self-confidence. In the years preceding the war he was one of an increasing number of people with an entrepreneurial spirit whose work, resourcefulness, and knowledge quickly brought them sizable wealth for the conditions in Bosnia at the time.

Dragan did not let work stand in the way of vacation and entertainment. He knew how to enjoy the fruits of his success. He often traveled abroad with his wife, who also worked in his firm. They spent part of the winter on the ski slopes in the mountains around Sarajevo and built a vacation home on one of the mountains where the 1984 Winter Olympics were held. They spent time during the summer in Dijana's parents' house on the island of Korcula. They would cruise around the nearby archipelago in their own boat and were gracious hosts on the terrace of their house with its wonderful view of the sea channel that separates Korcula Island from the Peljesac peninsula.

When the war began in Sarajevo in April 1992, Dragan became part of the Serbian Civic Forum; he was actually one of its founders. The Serbian Civic Forum was not a political party. It was formed by a group of Sarajevo Serbs who were not sympathizers of the Serbian Democratic Party (SDS), headed by Radovan Karadzic. The founders of the Serbian Civic Forum wanted to preserve multi-ethnic Sarajevo as much as they could and, in particular, through cooperation with the Bosnian Muslims, protect the Serbs who had not left Sarajevo. These Serbs, together with the other inhabitants of Sarajevo, were being subjected to constant bombing by Serbian artillery from the surrounding hills; as the war progressed they were also subjected to the increasing ill will and direct attacks of numerous Bosnian Muslim irregular police forces. The Muslim authorities in Sarajevo did not uphold some views and proclamations of the Serbian Civic Forum, but did not prohibit its work, either, since they welcomed the chance to show themselves before the world as advocates of a multi-ethnic Bosnia and Sarajevo. As the war proceeded, this Forum was increasingly marginalized and soon became politically and socially irrelevant.

In the besieged city, Dragan and Dijana shared the fate of the other Sarajevo inhabitants: they went into bomb-shelter basements when the shelling intensified, were greatly short of food, and managed to survive without water and electricity. During the second month of the war, I moved in with them since my apartment looked straight at a battery of Serbian artillery on Trebevic Hill. In those months together, we tremendously hated and cursed those on the surrounding hills who were destroying our lives, property, and our town.

Based on my own experience, during the first months of warfare the Bosnian Muslim authorities in Sarajevo demonstrated their great incompetence in managing town affairs, and, according to the accounts of other people who stayed in Sarajevo, this continued to the very end of the war. Among other things, they allowed a group of men who were repeat offenders to impose a true reign of terror in the town. The government not only gave them carte blanche but also extolled them. I could not remain uncritical of the serious mistakes and excesses by those who were in control of the town. This was not the case with Dragan, however. He simply would not allow anything to be said against the Bosnian Muslim leadership, although, it seemed to me he was aware that they were partially to blame for the increasingly difficult situation in Sarajevo. It was a taboo topic for him.

Several months after the beginning of warfare, Dijana managed to make it to her family's house on the island of Korcula. Along with many others who lived in Sarajevo, Dragan stayed in order to guard their apartment and tried to save at least part of the equipment from his private firm.

In the second year of the war Dragan received a summons from the Muslim authorities in Sarajevo to report to the detachment in charge of digging trenches around the town.

These trenches were to be used to defend Sarajevo. The job was considered highly risky and extremely dangerous. There were two reasons why the Serbs were an especially valued workforce to dig trenches. First, the longer the war lasted, the less confidence the Muslim-dominated government in Sarajevo had in the few Serbs who had openly or tacitly declared their loyalty to the Sarajevo authorities. From the point of view of security, it was better to employ the Serbs to dig trenches under Muslim supervision than to engage them in battle against their co-ethnics. Second, the trenches that were dug around Sarajevo were located right next to or on the very line that divided the Serbian armies and the army of Bosnia and Herzegovina. Thus, the trench diggers were the direct, visible, and practically unprotected target of the Serbian soldiers. The commanders of the Bosnian army did not expect the Serbs from enemy positions to fire on their fellow Serbs, so this is why they used them as the most suitable workforce to dig the trenches.

Naturally, efforts were made to let the Serbs on the other side know that if they fired they would be killing their co-ethnics. For this reason, the Serbs digging the trenches were often forced to establish verbal contact with their compatriots on the other side of the front (which was not hard since the warring parties were very close to each other), and begged them not to fire on them, their "brothers." There is no need to emphasize that, within the context of the extreme distrust between the Serbs and the Bosnian Muslims and the open condemnation of Serbs outside Sarajevo by those Serbs who remained in predominantly Muslim Sarajevo, the Serbs did not shrink from shooting at the nearest Bosnian army position, resulting in the death of a considerable number of trench diggers.

Dragan told me that the days he spent digging trenches were the most difficult in his life. The job was infinitely exhausting and his life was in danger. He firmly believed that he would not survive. He was saved by a physician who placed him in a hospital after establishing that Dragan's life truly was in great danger—from acute pneumonia. Under circumstances about which he does not want to speak, a year before the end of the war Dragan managed to leave Sarajevo and join Dijana on Korcula.

My wife and I were extremely pleased to learn that Dijana and Dragan were safe and sound on Korcula. We exchanged several letters and spoke on the phone, and then in 1998 we decided to visit Korcula. It seemed to us that they were as pleased as we were at the chance to see each other again.

After only a few days at their house on Korcula, it was clear to us that both Dragan's and Dijana's self-confidence and good mood had disappeared, particularly Dragan's. All the equipment from his firm in Sarajevo had been stolen, their foreign currency deposited in a Bosnian bank had been lost along with the bank, and their apartment and vacation house in territory controlled by Bosnian Serbs had been lost with their departure from Sarajevo. As a Serb, without Croatian citizenship, Dragan could not find work in Croatia, so they lived off the very low pension that Dijana had received in the meantime from Croatia. They sold their boat, since they could not maintain it, and every kuna (Croatian money) was precious. All in all, their low feelings were not the least bit strange. They shared the same fate as hundreds of thousands of refugees from the area of former Yugoslavia. But what was strange was Dragan's behavior.

During our two weeks on Korcula we spent most of our time with Dragan and Dijana, but we also spent quite a lot of time with a wider group of friends, which we were happy to note was highly ethnically mixed. Since the civil war in former Yugoslavia had ended three years previously, and we had all been its victims, some direct and some indirect, the people we socialized with that summer avoided the topic of inter-ethnic relations. All of us who met on the beach, in restaurants, in the evening around the TV (the world soccer championship was being broadcast) silently feared that if we were to start talking about ethnonational topics, about who started the war, which ethnonational group had suffered the most, etc., we would most certainly become estranged and might even argue.

Everyone but Dragan. Almost every chance he got, when there was a reason and when there was no reason at all, Dragan would attack the Serbs at great length: the Serbs from Bosnia, the Serbs from Croatia, the Serbs from Serbia. He said the Serbs were solely to blame for the recently ended war, that the Serbs were a genocidal people who could not be trusted either in times of peace or war and were to be avoided like the plague. He said it with great bitterness, without the slightest concealment of his hatred for the Serbs. If he mentioned the Croats and Bosnian Muslims, he would say they were the sole and exclusive victims, which meant that they should be forgiven for anything bad they had done during the war. As a rule, no one in our crowd reacted to Dragan's persistently repeated disparagement of the Serbs. Those present would keep silent a few moments after Dragan's bilious tirades, and then conversation would continue where it had stopped.

Dragan used every topic of conversation to express quite clearly his opinions of the Serbs. For example, if I referred in conversation to something I had read in the Belgrade magazines *Vreme* or *Nin*, which were openly opposed to Milosevic's regime, Dragan would cut me off. He claimed there was not a single opposition newspaper or electronic media in Belgrade and in all of Serbia, that all the Serbs without exception were nationalist hardliners. That was simply the way it was: end of discussion.

Once when I told him that he should go and see about his vacation house on Jahorina Mountain and ask whether anyone wanted to buy it, because regardless of what he got for it the money would mean a lot to him in their difficult financial situation, he replied that he would never step onto territory controlled by the Serbs. Later I learned of another manifestation of Dragan's changed behavior that simply shocked me.

Before my wife and I arrived on Korcula, Dragan's brother had died in Novi Sad, in Serbia. Dragan did not go to the funeral. First, he considered that his brother had not been critical enough of the Serbs, and second, his hatred of the Serbs would not let him go to their territory, even for a day or two to attend his brother's funeral.

Whenever we were alone, I would speak to my wife about Dragan's behavior. It was so different from that of everyone else we socialized with that summer that it was hard to pass over it in silence. As much as we tried to find an explanation for Dragan's behavior, we also wondered why no one from our group countered his outpouring of hatred towards the Serbs, why no one reacted.

Although we could not find a common reason for the lack of reaction to Dragan's completely biased verbal attacks against the Serbs, because there were certainly many reasons—fear of being considered a Serbophile, which was a very undesirable label in Tudjman's Croatia; opportunism; avoiding painful discussions on sensitive topics, and so on—Dragan's attitude towards the Serbs should nonetheless be explained. It was so conspicuous, stood out so clearly in the group we spent time with that summer on Korcula, and clashed so glaringly with Dragan's earlier, primarily Yugoslav, orientation, which made no distinction between the peoples of the second Yugoslavia. Of course, valid arguments could be given for the opinion that Milosevic's regime was the most to blame for the recent war in the Balkans, that the Serbian side—particularly at the beginning of the war when it was far better armed—inflicted the greatest damage and committed the worst crimes. But it is one thing to look more or less objectively at what actually happened in the second Yugoslavia from the end of the 1980s to the mid-1990s, with all possible subjective digressions caused by the scope of personal and family loss, and it is another thing to be extremely biased and accuse only one side for all the atrocities committed during the war, as well as speak of evil being inborn in a people, their genocidal tendencies, and so on.

What attracted the most attention in Dragan's impassioned Serbophobia was not his completely uncritical or biased views, since the last dozen years have produced a substantially large number of inhabitants of the second Yugoslavia with similar views. Nor was it the fact that the target of Dragan's hatred was his own people, which is an extremely rare case in areas torn by ethnonationalistic passions and ideas. Rather, it was his intrusive, repeated, indiscriminate attacks on all Serbs without exception, not spurred by the topic or conversation or current events. Knowing that during the war he had actually suffered the most at the hands of the Bosnian Muslim government—who had taken away his apartment, stolen the equipment from his firm, forced him in his later years to do the extremely exhausting and dangerous job of digging trenches, and prevented him from leaving Sarajevo when he decided to leave—he could have been expected to turn his sharp tongue against the Bosnian Muslim leadership, in addition to the Serbs, whom he considered exclusively to blame for the war. This, however, was not the case. It seemed as though some internal force was impelling Dragan to announce whenever he could, wherever he was, just how much he abhorred the Serbs. This internal force, which made his behavior seem unnatural and lacking spontaneity, not the least free, requires an explanation.

Dragan believed he could not return to Sarajevo since he had nowhere to live. His apartment had been taken away. If there was a need for the services that his private firm offered, he would have to invest in new equipment and he did not have the money. Even if he'd had the money, his chances as a Serb of developing a business in Sarajevo were quite small. Sarajevo was becoming more and more ethnically homogeneous with each passing day and was more than ninety percent Muslim. There was no question of his going to Serbia. Practically speaking, the only place he had to live was on

Korcula, in Croatia, where his wife had a pension and where he also hoped to receive a Croatian pension, which did happen later. So he had to accept the fact that he would most likely spend the rest of his life on Korcula in Croatia.

Faced with such prospects, he had to show and prove to all those around him, almost on a daily basis, that he, although a Serb, fostered antagonistic feelings towards the Serbs. In that extremely important regard in ethnic times—that is, one's attitude towards the members of rival ethnic groups— he shared the views of the party in power in Croatia, and of a considerable number of the Croats. He actually shared his understanding of those views. To be as convincing as possible in his own eyes and in the eyes of those around him, he had to go one step or even several steps farther than the attitude towards the Serbs that was prevalent in the Croatia of that time. He had to do it as a Serb, who was not expected to be a Serbophobe in the twilight of civil war, just as the Croats in Serbia, in the same circumstances, were not expected to throw stick and stones at other Croats. The Serb in Croatia and the Croat in Serbia wanted the approval of their fellow citizens, wanted to atone for the fact they belonged to their vile people, and prevent or at least mitigate the hostility to which they might be exposed by the ethnically dominant population.

With his intrusive disparagement of the Serbs, this is most likely what Dragan, consciously or unconsciously, wanted to achieve. His behavior reflected the magnitude of the internal and external pressure to which he was exposed. The internal pressure was caused by the fear that he would be exiled from his new environment, that he would be treated like an intruder, or, in the worst case, that his life would be endangered; the external pressure was formed by the ethnonationalistic passions of the environment in which he lived. His conspicuous and overemphasized attacks against the members of his own ethnonational group might also have been intended to quiet the conscious or unconscious voice inside him that told him there was something unseemly in what he was saying. Or perhaps he believed that the Serbs would resent him, or even take revenge on him, because of his active support of the Serbian Civic Forum, which has been viewed by many Serbs as a treacherous activity intended to appease the Bosnian Muslims in Sarajevo.

I wonder whether Dragan's described behavior, this defensive attitude of a man in danger that he exhibited even in Sarajevo and developed completely in Croatia, can be understood as mimicry, a type of adaptation, an expression of man's primordial instinct for survival—one of the side effects of ethnic times. In other words, can Dragan's behavior in Croatia be viewed as functional, almost expected and therefore normal behavior in ethnic times, when the law of the majority becomes inexorable and every individual difference, particularly of an ethnic nature, endangers one's life?

Ethnic times are usually spoken of as being unambiguous, as times in which it is easy to predict people's behavior, views and beliefs. This is clearly not always the case. Ethnic times also generate seemingly paradoxical changes in people. Dragan taught me that the ethnonationalism of an ethnonational group is spawned not only by ethnonationalistic feelings and views towards members of other ethnonational groups. It was clear from Dragan's example that ethnonationalism can also be produced by what I would call *inverse ethnonationalism*: exaggerated, impassioned hatred of the members of one's own race, accompanied by a completely uncritical attitude towards the ethnonationalism of those living in the environment in which the inverse ethnonationalist now lives.

The Woes of Divided Loyalty

Children from ethnonationally mixed marriages are the greatest victims of times in which ethnonationalistic views and feelings rule people's hearts and minds. I will try to show how and why by first recalling the objective status, or rather the negation of the status, of such children in ethnonationalistic times, and then pointing out some of the empirical, experiential sides of the world of children who are the fruit of love between parents of different ethnonational origin.

Ethnonationalism, lest we forget, requires the individual to identify with his/her ethnonational group. It demands unsolicited emotional attachment to the group; in the process, loyalty to one's own ethnonational group must surpass all other forms of attachments and loyalties.

Relations among people who are defined by ethnonationalism are based primarily on attributed rather than acquired characteristics. Ethnonationalism-defined relations are ethnic, not national. All other elements in this type of relationship and how strongly they are represented result from the element of attribution. Not even the best pretext will help someone free himself/herself from strictly respecting the obligations he or she has taken on, or been forced to take on, for his/her own ethnonational group.

Relations arising from attributed statuses are highly binding, although they do not result from free individual choice. Or, perhaps they are binding for this very reason. A person cannot choose his/her parents and gender, for example. Can ethnonationality be freely chosen? This question should be reformulated: first, can one choose one's ethnic affiliation? And second, can one choose one's national affiliation?

We should bear in mind that ethnic identity is exclusive, which means it can only be acquired by birth. National identity is inclusive; in other words, it can be acquired, for example, by living a certain number of years in some (national) state. Ethnic identity is pre-political and national affiliation is political. So if we understand nationality in the ethnic manner as affiliation to a group whose members have the same origin—which ethnonationalists constantly emphasize either openly or implicitly—then we can say that the link among people of the same ethnonationality is exclusive. Those without the same ethnic affiliation cannot be part of it. If, however, national identity is defined in the legal sense, in the sense of citizenship, then the individual's relationship towards people of the same nationality cannot be called exclusive. Nationality in the non-ethnic sense can be acquired; it is not acquired automatically, by order of an attributed status. Indeed, in a significantly large number of countries nationality (of a specific national state) is acquired by being born on the soil of that state. This form of acquiring nationality might also be considered a social relationship that results from attributed status (just as with gender and parents, a person cannot choose where he will be born), but in another (geographical-state-administrative) sense and not ethno-biological-cultural.

What about the ethnonational identity or affiliation of children from ethnonationally mixed marriages? Common sense tells us that they should have the freedom to choose their ethnonationality. However, the assumption that children from ethnonationally mixed marriages should have the freedom to choose their ethnonationality negates the essence of ethnonationality—its exclusiveness as an attribute acquired by birth. (The automatic, implicit attribution of the father's ethnonationality to children from ethnonationally mixed marriages, which is the unwritten rule in some environments and the written rule in others, results from patriarchal conventions and runs counter to the logic of biology, which ethnonationalists like to cite. It is a generally known fact that both parents have an equal share in determining the child's genetic "material.")

Does the freedom to choose their ethnonationality mean that children from an ethnonationally mixed marriage can choose either the ethnonationality of the mother or that of the father? Or do they have a third option of having both the mother's and father's ethnonationality at the same time? The answer to this last question is that they can in the national but not in the ethnic sense. In other words, the child of an Englishwoman and a Frenchman can and cannot be both a Frenchman and an Englishman. It all depends on whether the emphasis is put on ethnicity or nationality in ethnonationality.

Ethnic affiliation is all that counts for ethnonationalists. Thus, it is no wonder that they consider children from ethnonationally different parents to be freaks, bastards, ethnonational anomalies. From the viewpoint of the ethnonationalist, the children of ethnonationally different parents do not exist. Ethnonationality to the ethnonationalist is such an all-consuming characteristic that not having it, or not having it in a pure, unequivocal form and in sufficient amount, is the same as not being a man in "the true sense of the word." Questions such as, "What is the ethnic affiliation of a child whose mother and father are from parents of different ethnic origin?" infuriate them to no end.

In this environment, children from ethnically mixed marriages are marginalized, unrecognized, maligned, wretched, the object of general derision and even hatred. Through no fault of their own, people from such an origin feel excommunicated externally and divided internally, faced with the urgency of making a decision which, regardless of what it is, will be coerced, unnatural. And so, we ask, how do "ethnic crossbreeds" cope with the internal tension that results from being "homeless?" Each responds to the woes of divided loyalty in his/her own way, although there are several more characteristic types of response.

1. During epidemic ethnonationalism, a number of people from ethnonationally mixed marriages rapidly leave an environment in which the population has started to divide itself on the basis of ethnic affiliation. They are certainly not the only ones to leave such a sociopolitical environment but, I would say, they are the first and most numerous among those who leave of their own free will. They seem to be the most sensitive to changes in society presaged by strict ethnonational divisions. Since they cannot and/or do not want to choose their ethnonationality, they move to regions where, as they like to say, they can belong to no one and be mostly themselves. It is interesting that when they are outside the sphere of influence of ethnonationalism, they are inclined to socialize with one another, create attachments and some sort of separate community, or special ethnic group. (It is a little known fact that on the island of Mauritius children from mixed marriages are considered a separate ethnic group.) They feel so different from all others that in a new environment, where people's ethnic affiliation is not given a lot of attention, they feel most comfortable when they are with others like themselves.

2. The second possibility open to people from ethnically mixed marriages during times of nationalistic high tide is to withdraw into what has been called *internal emigration.*

They simply hold their tongue and make no ethnonational display. Confused and frightened, they are mostly preoccupied with being seen and heard as little as possible. They act as though they understand that they simply do not have the right to many things.

3. The third way of trying to solve the woes of divided loyalty is to accept the ethnonationality of one of the parents. This most often does not go unpunished. Depending on upbringing, internal family dynamics, and so on, however close a child from an ethnonationally heterogeneous marriage feels to the ethnonational matrix of one of the parents—thus making it easier for him in ethnonational times to pronounce himself a member of one specific ethnic community—that child cannot completely silence the voice of the myths, beliefs, habits, and so on, of the cultural-ethnic identity of the other parent. Inside himself, the child does not feel a dyed-in-the-wool member of the ethnonational community he or she has opted for, but neither is he or she a complete deserter from culture of the rejected and repudiated ethnonational group. Thus, the child must put full stress on his/her chosen identity. He or she not only denies any links with the ethnonational community of one parent, but also disparages, persecutes, and even destroys the members of that community. He or she behaves just like most ardent ethnonationalists. On the one hand they aggrandize their ethnonational group and proudly exclaim that they are happy there is nothing in their family from "that other side." On the other hand they disparage everything that is not his/her ethnonationally authentic expression and resolve to eradicate those who might endanger the "purity" of their ethnonationality. History has shown quite a few tyrants who zealously and systematically harmed members of the ethnonational group of one of their parents.

4. A number of children from ethnically mixed marriages, pressured by the imperative of the times to be "either-or," solve the problem by rising above the dilemma. They refuse to accept that their parents' opposing ethnonationalities

have nothing in common, that they are completely alien, removed from each other. They find common denominators between the ethnonational communities of their parents, which are not hard to find in most cases, and proclaim them extremely important values that reconcile or, more exactly lay to rest, most of the real and invented incompatibilities and antagonisms between the ethnonational communities. For example, children who resort to this mechanism when one parent is a Croat and the other a Serb alleviate the woes of divided loyalty by stressing that regardless of their current quarrels, both the Croats and the Serbs are Christians, a characteristic that is much more important and crucial than all their disagreements. Regardless of the accuracy of this affirmation, it can help a Serbo-Croatian (or Croato-Serbian) child survive in nationalistic times and remain open to the ethnocultural matrix of both parents.

5. Finally, a number of children from mixed marriages manage to avoid bowing to either side by choosing both sides, either openly or in secret. For example, some "ethnic crossbreeds" manage to "adapt" their ethnonational identity to the environment in which they currently find themselves. Surrounded by Croats, they say they are Croats, and in the company of Serbs no one is allowed to doubt that the "Serbian half" of their ethnic baggage is incomparably greater. Or in public they present themselves as "unmistakable Serbs" and succeed, but mostly on the sly, in doing business with the Croats whose characteristics and customs are close to the "Croatian half" of their ethnonational being.

This last form of coping with the demands of an environment having highly stressed ethnonational divisions can give the impression of misusing double ethnic origin. I, however, look at it as a clever negation of fundamental ethnonationalistic principles, turning a seeming drawback into a real advantage. Such an outward misuse of one's ethnically mixed origins is actually the triumph of personal freedom over collective rigidity. Since the children are "ethnic anomalies" and "ethnic crossbreeds," they have shown themselves capable of making a strong blow against ethnonational prejudices—and of toying with these prejudices when it suits them.

Ethnonationalism in the Genes

In ethnonationalistic times, there is unmistakable familiarity among members of the same ethnic group. They are, of course, on familiar terms with one another even when ethnonationalism does not hold sway in their hearts and minds, particularly when they live among foreigners. But this phenomenon is more evident in ethnonationalistic times, especially in an ethnonationally heterogeneous environment. It's interesting to observe then what happens among people who have never met before and most likely will not in the future—people who are not connected by the same or similar professions, by class or family ties, or the same hobby. When these people, who have absolutely nothing in common except the same ethnonationality meet by chance at the same party, on the same train, in line, or anywhere, they address and treat one another like old acquaintances and old buddies. In a twinkling they find a common language, find that they have the same interests and views, complete spiritual and mental kinship, and even identity. The biological identity seems to go without saying.

Are people of the same ethnonationality truly kin? When their leaders address them as "brothers" and "sisters," particularly in ethnonationalistic times, are they actually reminding them of a fact that people have simply forgotten? When ethnonationalistic views and beliefs are being disseminated, people of the same ethnonationality are turned much more towards each other, protecting and helping; concurrently, they disparage and detest people from other ethnic groups much more than at other times. Is this perhaps what prompts people from the same ethnic group to believe they truly have some blood ties?

The answers to all these questions can be found in the work of sociobiologists. They claim that the cause of ethnonationalistic, ethnocentric, and tribal behavior is found in the genes and thus has a biological foundation. Where does the biological basis for ethno-nationalism come from? They claim that the behavioral pattern of *brotherhood inside- animosity outside*, which is so characteristic of ethnonationalists, was shown to have the greatest adaptive potential during prehistorical and historical times. In other words, those who overvalued their own group and sacrificed themselves willingly for it, while demonstrating hostile feelings towards members of other groups, had the greatest ability to adapt. Apparently only those tribes whose ranks had the greatest number of altruists in this sense of the word were able to survive.

Sociobiologists' views seem accurate if we understand altruism as solidarity, providing assistance to people in trouble regardless of the direct benefit that might result from it. However, according to sociobiologists, altruism is behavior that increases the reproductive capability of others at the expense of decreasing these same capabilities among the altruists. In other words, if, acting altruistically, altruists considerably decrease their own reproductive capabilities, then over time they inevitably decrease the number of genes that favor altruistic behavior or are the basis for such behavior. It turns out, then, that altruists do not have great adaptive potential; quite the contrary, their adaptive potential would be very small, since they would be condemned to die out over the long or short run. Over time the number of people with "altruistic genes" would decrease.

Sociobiologists, however, claim that "altruistic genes" are not really in danger, since altruistic behavior is in the service of "gene selfishness" or the product of simple profit considerations, as Pierre van den Berghe (1981), one of the leading representatives of this line of thinking in social-psychology (and biology) emphasizes. Since the basic interest of genes is to survive and multiply—which should be one of the basic laws in the so-called natural world—genes favor all forms of nepotistic, tribal, ethnocentric, nationalistic behavioral patterns that encourage sacrificing oneself for others who have the same genetic makeup as the "altruists." In this way, in spite of their personal sacrifice—or perhaps for that very reason—the number of altruists, or "altruistic genes," increases rather than decreases.

Speaking in the language of genetics, brothers and sisters are closer to one another than parents are to their children. What does this mean in practical terms? If the natural or nature-given instinct is to multiply and reproduce, to increase the number of one's own genes and transfer them to one's offspring, then people are closer to satisfying that instinct when they sacrifice themselves for their brothers and sisters than when they fight to preserve their own existence and try (as much as possible) to reproduce themselves. Their own reproduction can never have such a great effect as sacrificing themselves for others who have a similar genetic makeup. This inclusive fitness ("my characteristics are transferred to collateral kin") has a greater effect on enabling the survival of the super-family, tribe, or ethnic group than the ability to reproduce. The essence of tribalism, ethnocentrism, and ethnonationalism would thus be the superiority of inclusive fitness—as shown by the number of one's own genes that are included in the next generation—over reproductive fitness—which means the number of one's direct descendants. Therefore, tribal and ethnonationalistic mentality would be the triumph of unnamed biological forces within man, or more accurately, over man. In accordance with that, all endeavors to eliminate such a mentality, dull its cutting edge, prevent its impact on society and on relations among people, particularly among ethnic groups, would be futile.

Some characteristics of the tribal mentality, indeed, speak on behalf of its inevitability, which means its biological foundation. This mentality is easier to arouse, mobilize, and turn instrumental as needed than the mentality linked to that of belonging to the same class, political party, union, etc. Even more important, should the tribal mentality come into conflict with the mentality linked to the above forms of association and affiliation, the outcome is almost always known in advance. The tribal mentality will win. Furthermore, the implicit brutality of conflicts caused by the tribal mentality is immeasurable compared to that in class, party, or neighborhood conflicts. Finally, the tribal mentality has more of the irrational in it than the mentality that results from class, party, professional, sports, neighborhood, etc., affiliations—if the latter have anything at all irrational in them. This irrationality in the tribal mentality, something that is impervious to rational arguments, implies its extra-awareness—i.e. biological foundation.

What, if anything, speaks against the above sociobiological views, questions their basic thesis that ethnonationalistic behavior is in our genes? If we set aside the extremely complex question of the relationship between genes and behavior, regardless of its essential importance for sociobiological argument, the following questions cannot be avoided: How do altruists in the above sense—that is, those who sacrifice themselves for the survival of others who have more or less the same genetic makeup as they do—know that those they have laid down their lives for are truly related to them, regardless of how distantly? What is the basis for this knowledge? By the same culture, same customs, language, the names they bear, and god to whom they pray is one of the possible answers. Sharing these characteristics, however, provides neither proof nor guarantee that all those people also have the same genetic makeup that a correlation exists between people's cultural and biological characteristics.

Conscious of the gravity of this last question, van den Berghe points out that ethnocentrism developed during millions or hundreds of thousands of years of evolution as a prolongation or continuation of sacrificing for one's kin. It does not seem so important that sacrificing oneself for one's kin was sometimes taken more for granted than actually carried out. Importance lies in the fact that there was close enough kinship for there to be a basis for the powerful feelings that we call nationalism, tribalism, racism, ethnocentrism.

What does this mean in practical terms? Sacrificing oneself for one's kinsmen, for people with the same genetic makeup, was biologically justified in the distant past when people, it is assumed, lived in large groups (superfamilies, clans). It was justified in the light of the biological-evolutionary imperative that the same genes should multiply and spread, that their life should be prolonged. Nepotistic behavior made sense then since it truly resulted in the multiplication and prolongation of the same genetic base. However, once these primordial groups began to multiply and their members intermingled, the belief that the members of the new communities originated from the same ancestors and were therefore blood relatives became primarily the subject of myths presented for the sake of maintaining group cohesion. That brought an end to the biological-evolutionary justification of tribal behavior, and particularly the ethnonationalistic behavior that came later.

Is holding on to some type of behavior even though what originally motivated it has disappeared an example of what famed psychologist Gordon Allport (1946) called "functional autonomy of the motivation"? People used to kill wild animals for food in order to survive. Today they go hunting for enjoyment, and providing food for survival is the last thing on their minds.

Is the belief in a common ancestor or ancestors that is so carefully maintained and fostered among the members of the same ethnic (ethnonational) group dependent on allegedly unique cultural traits that do not have and cannot have the inexorable, unquestionable, untouchable, almost unworldly quality that goes along with what has been biologically given? The specific cultural features of the members of an ethnic or ethnonational group are nonetheless something arbitrary, a question of valuation, a subjective judgment rather than something that is objectively given, that is beyond all doubt. So it was necessary to call upon the group's biological features as the reason for extolling "our people" and disparaging and even exterminating "the others." Regardless of how much ethnonationalists today center their arguments on the defense of their own cultural idiom, the belief in a common ancestor, which means the cultural ties of all members of the ethnonational group, is one of the myths that ethnonationalists have the hardest time renouncing.

Finally, the biological foundation or significance of ethnonational behavior can be viewed from a somewhat different aspect than that familiar to sociobiologists. Assuming that members of the group have blood ties, the idea might sound convincing that tribal behavior and unrestricted sacrifice for "my people" results in the enlargement of the group and the survival of its members, who are "my kind." But it is also true that the tribal, ethnonationalistic behavior of the members of a community sooner or later endangers that same community as a whole and threatens its physical existence. This at least is what the experience of history teaches us. Communities with the greatest number of extreme altruists, who are still called heroes, are not communities with a highly certain future.

WORKS CITED

Allport, G. *Personality: A psychological interpretation*. New York: Holt, 1946.

Van den Berghe, P. *The ethnic phenomenon*. New York: Elsevier, 1981.

Brief Conversation with an Ethnonationalist about Children from Ethnically Mixed Marriages

Ethnonationalist: I wonder what children from ethnically mixed marriages are doing in these strange times, when we're all splitting up, or others are splitting us up, I can't tell anymore. Whose side are they on, their father's or their mother's?

Interviewer: It depends on how they themselves feel. Whether they feel more at home in the culture of their mother or father, since ethnonational sentiment is first and foremost a matter of self-perception.

Ethnonationalist: All I can say is that since earliest times our children have been raised in the spirit of the traditions and culture of their father. Some say that is because our culture is patriarchal, and they usually think this is something bad, just like the whole world is writing bad things about us now. I personally think that our culture is good, better than many other cultures that are fashionable today. And not just because it's ours. Regardless of whether we call it patriarchal or something else.

Interviewer: In patriarchal cultures the father is the main figure in handling family affairs, raising children, etc. In today's world, however, this is less and less the case since women have an increasing role in society in general, and thus in handling family affairs. This is why patriarchal cultures are old-fashioned, not to say a thing of the past. Finally, regardless of the dominant type of culture, mothers are closer to children in their early developmental period, and are thus able to pass on the customs, habits, language, etc., of their ethnonational group to their children more than fathers.

Ethnonationalist: In that case, that is, if, as you claim, both parents participate equally in bringing up their children, then, as far as I understand raising children, the parent with the stronger personality has the greater influence. Just look at any group. Individuals with strong personalities impose themselves on others and serve as their role model. That's the way it is with people, and I think with animals, too. They all want to be like the strongest one, the main one leading the others. I don't see why it should be any different in a family. As far as I know—which I allow that maybe you don't—people from our culture, both men and women, have especially strong personalities.

Is There Something Mentally Wrong with Ethnonationalists?

Nationalists' behavior, particularly their argumentation and exclusionist nature, is astonishing, to say the least, to people who have different ethnonationalistic views and beliefs. The astonishment is all the greater if a person's nationalistic turnabout has come suddenly—almost overnight—as is often the case. When the use of force begins and warfare of broader proportions breaks out inspired by ethnonationalism, the extremely militant and often criminal behavior of ethnonationalists frequently leads to the question: Are these people sane, or is there something wrong with them?

Although the ethnonationalistic pattern of behavior and manner of reasoning, viewed externally, have some similarities with the (psycho)pathological, ethnonationalists, to set the record straight, are not mentally disturbed. What we are dealing with is the behavior and manner of thinking and feeling that is shared by a large number, and even most people in a community during epidemic nationalism. This behavioral pattern becomes widespread in ethnic times and is actually how ethnonationalism is asserted. A distinction must be made between this type of ethnonationalistic behavior and that of endemic ethnonationalists—people who advocate nationalistic views and beliefs almost their whole lives, even when such views are not the social norm or a desirable form of social behavior. Epidemic nationalists are of principal importance to society, since it is only when ethnonationalism takes on the proportions of a widespread social movement that it is able to influence what happens in society and change social reality. Any ethnonationalism outside of a collective phenomenon has no great social relevance.

Therefore, when discussing whether there is something mentally wrong with ethnonationalists, the real question is: Can the specific behavior and manner of thinking and feeling of people who demonstrate ethnonationalistic views and beliefs for a short period in their lives, along with the greater part of their community, be considered mentally sound?

Because ethnonationalism is a collective phenomenon—a specific form of behaving, thinking, and feeling that is not limited to individual existence but is recognized as being common to a great number and even the greatest number of people in society—does not allow us to see it as a psychopathological manifestation. The collective nature of ethnonationalism is not the only reason, but it is certainly one of the basic and even most important reasons why ethnonationalists cannot be considered mentally disturbed. Mental disturbance is connected to individual existence and simply does not exist outside of it. The best way to understand the magnitude of the difference between collective, ostensibly pathological behavior such as that found in ethnonationalists, and the individual pathological episode or mentally disturbed person, is to compare their basic characteristics.

Any form of collective behavior is contingent on specific social circumstances and processes that are recognizable and can be relatively easily determined. Social poverty of broad proportions; a universal feeling of uncertainty, expectation, hopelessness, fear; people's artificially created or well-founded belief that they are in imminent danger from some serious infectious disease, the punishment of God, the supernatural, members of another community (another ethnonational collective, for example); the appearance of a charismatic leader who shows the road to salvation, the way out of the current situation which is hard to bear—these are all circumstances that create fertile ground for the expansion of a uniform pattern of behavior among most members of a community, for their being part of the "common lot."

These circumstances by themselves, without the participation of biological, individual-psychological factors, create some sort of collective proclivity for the emergence of a behavioral pattern that is common to most of the community members. On the other hand, these same circumstances and the corresponding state of the "collective soul" do not give rise to individual mental disturbance. Individual psychopathology originates on a terrain that is formed more or less simultaneously and equally by the biological, psychological and social elements of someone's existence. The nature of the dynamic connections among these elements is primarily unknown to us, and as a rule differs from one person to the next.

If most members of a community have some common characteristic—for example, the same ethnic origin, same religion, the same or similar system of beliefs and values, common history, collective memory— they quickly and easily form a collective predisposition to uniform behavior, reasoning, and feeling. The same thing happens when most members of a community receive information about socially relevant events from the same source: their views, and even their feelings, not only become uniform, but their communication with each other is facilitated. They have fewer and fewer disagreements, if any, since their views are almost identical on the important aspects of their daily lives and of the group to which they belong. These factors that help create a predisposition among community members to adopt a common behavioral pattern, broadly speaking, have practically no effect on individual psychopathological manifestations, and least of all on the creation of conditions for their appearance.

Since ethnonationalism is a collective phenomenon, its actors greatly resemble one another in terms of their behavior, the ideas they represent, and the arguments they use. This is nowhere near the case with individual psychopathological manifestations. Mentally disturbed people, even when suffering from the same disturbance, are quite different. In short, psychopathological expression differs from one person to another.

What effect does collective behavior of any kind have on the group, on the collective? It homogenizes the group. Mentally disturbed behavior, however, destroys the cohesion of the group: it is socially aberrant and clashes with the socially expected form of behavior. Furthermore, it represents an unreasonable and unintelligible form of behavior, which is why customary measures—the principle of punishment and reward in particular—cannot "make it toe the line," conform to the social norm.

Do those who are under the sway of collective behavior complain about it? Do they wish to free themselves from it because it bothers them in one way or another, interferes with their daily lives, their jobs? No, practically never. I have never met a single ethnonationalist who complained that he didn't feel well because he was an ethnonationalist and/or inquired whether there was any way to help him stop being an ethnonationalist. Mentally disturbed people, on the other hand, most certainly complain and seek help. They complain that they can't sleep, that they have lost the will to live, that they hear someone calling them when there's not a soul around, that they are hypertense the whole day long, and so on. It must be said, though, that the mentally disturbed do not always complain and do not always look for help. This happens, for example, when they are completely uncritical, when they lack any sort of insight into their true state. But this is a rather rare occurrence among the overall mass of mentally disturbed.

What can mitigate the manifestation of a collective form of behavior or cause it to recede? First of all, the disappearance of those same social circumstances that helped create the collective readiness for its formation can cause it to recede. As far as individual psychopathology is concerned, changes in general social circumstances have little or no effect. Psychic suffering caused by mental disorder can be mitigated primarily or solely by individualized, specific therapeutic procedures.

Finally, once the collective behavioral pattern has withdrawn from the social scene, when it ceases to be a dominant form of social behavior, it leaves no trace on its former participants. They continue to live as though nothing had happened, relying on their own devices, as though until recently they had not been under the sway of an idea, a special way of looking at themselves and others, which they had shared with most of the community members. This is completely different with the mentally disturbed. With slight exaggeration, it could be said that after having been treated for or cured of a mental disorder, not a single person is the same as before he or she became disturbed. Sometimes only the disturbed individual feels this, but it can at times be obvious to those closest to him/her or to those who only know him/her superficially.

I have focused on a comparison between the collective and individual psychopathological in order to show as convincingly as possible how they differ. A highly visible line must be drawn between what is *bad* and what is *mad*. If this is not done, we might attach the label of mentally disturbed upon members of those groups which, for any reason, are resolute in their intention to destroy people of a different ethnic origin. This would confuse mental disturbance—which is, I repeat, primarily an individual disorder—with what primarily concerns group happenings and moral considerations. As a result, psychiatric diagnostics and classification, and even psychiatry itself, would become superfluous. Of far greater consequence, however, is that if we lump together those people who blindly bow to ruling ideas, those who uncritically submit to national and ethnonational authority, those who follow commands coming from *blood* and *soil* with those who have hallucinations and those who have delusions, we are in danger of treating them all the same way and of trying to prevent the above phenomena with more or less the same procedures and activities. If we do that we would be doing wrong to both the mentally ill and to those who take part in collective crimes inspired by ethnonational convictions.

Of course, not all ethnonationalists who have the lives of innocent people on their conscience will be unhappy if they are declared out of their minds, particularly if they are charged with the crimes they have committed. I have been receiving an increasing amount of information about a small number of psychiatrists in some of the states formed after the disintegration of the second Yugoslavia who in recent years have been inclined to declare people who have committed heinous crimes inspired by ethnonationalism as insufficiently accountable or irresponsible, thus saving them from the punishment they deserve. These lines are intended above all for their eyes.

Why Ethnonationalists
Are Aggressive

The very mention of the word ethnonationalism brings to mind violence, looting, fanaticism, conflicts, intolerance. Does ethnonationalism really have to be militant and lead to conflicts not only between rival ethnonational groups but also within communities where the spirit of ethnonationalism holds sway? Before I explain the affirmative answer, I would like to recall the difference between aggressiveness and aggression. Aggressiveness denotes aggressive potential, which depends on how much desire, need, and impulse a man has to act aggressively. Aggression is the expression of aggressiveness: it is aggressiveness transformed into concrete action.

Dormant tension is an integral part of intergroup relations. In times of social strain, competition, and instability, ethnonationalist leaders play on this latent opposition among groups, striving to convert it into open inter-ethnic hostility and violence. "The self-assertion of 'We are,' with its potential for confrontation with 'We are' of other groups, is *in-*

herently a carrier of aggression, together with the consequent fears of persecution, and is thus always attended by a sense of risk, a potential for violence" (Kakar, 1996: 189).

Ethnonationalism increases the aggressive potential in people. It also hastens aggression. In other words, people whose hearts and minds have been won over by ethnonationalistic views and beliefs are more prepared to act aggressively than those who do not hold to the spirit of ethnonationalism; ethnonationalists in any case act more aggressively than those who are not ethnonationalists.

Ethnonationalistic feelings and views are always accompanied by people's dissatisfaction with the economic state of their ethnonational group, dissatisfaction with the amount of freedom they have, the rights they can exercise, the future that awaits them, their children, or their children's children if nothing changes. Of course, were they to be asked, an extremely small number of people would readily reply that they are completely satisfied with themselves and with their economic situation, human rights, and the development level of democracy in their environment.

This dissatisfaction becomes inexorably greater and more pointed when someone tells you that a very specific culprit is to blame for you and your ethnonational community's rather unenviable state. Up until then you have been vaguely dissatisfied, both reconciled and unreconciled to the current situation; you both accept it and feel it should be improved, but you aren't quite sure what should be done to make tomorrow better than today.

When people from your ethnic group, whom you are mostly inclined to believe, start repeating through the media that you and your compatriots are not living better for a very specific reason—a rival ethnonational group—your dissatisfaction and your aggressiveness considerably increase. A recognizable, visible explanation appears for your misfortunes, poverty, and relative lack of freedom, and you thus receive a concrete reason to be dissatisfied. Now you know you are dissatisfied because people from another ethnic group are preventing you and your compatriots from living the way you should; you are dissatisfied because nothing is being done to impede, thwart, incapacitate those who are to blame for your unsatisfactory state. And this is exactly what your ethnonational leader will tell you next: "All of 'us,'" he or she will say, "should do everything in 'our' power, the sooner the better, to stop the members of the rival ethnonational group from acting against 'our' interests; we should remove them from 'our' environment, isolate them, denounce them, put them in the pillory." Thus a rise in ethnonationalism is accompanied not only by a rise in people's aggressive potential, but also in their aggression which is directed, channeled against members of a rival ethnonational community.

Aggressiveness and aggression are given additional encouragement by the glorification of those individuals who have proved to be especially effective in "silencing" members of the rival ethnic group, destroying them and their property, which should represent the punishment they deserve for all the evil they have done to "us" in the past and would most certainly continue to do had they not been prevented in time. In ethnonationalistic times serial killers, those who have difficulty controlling their aggressive impulses, sadists, and offenders of all types become people of high standing. To be a true member of your ethnic group you have to be like them, act like them, and reason like them; you are thereby helping to protect and develop your own ethnonational collective. The people who become a model of behavior have a hard time controlling their impulses, have almost no idea what it means to be in a dilemma, haven't the slightest doubt about the rightness for the job they are devoted to: mistreating, torturing, and killing people from a rival ethnonational group, expelling them, destroying all traces of their existence in a specific territory. By emulating such "authentic defenders" of ethnonational interests, people become more aggressive and incomparably more inclined to aggression than when other role models hold sway on the public stage.

As soon as a rival ethnonational group has been declared the greatest hindrance to "our" development and freedom, and people's aggressiveness (regardless of its origin) and aggression are directed at the members of that specific ethnonational group, all of this group's activities are interpreted as malicious, directed against "us," intended to undermine "our" economic power, belittle "our" culture, desecrate "our" saints, and prevent the freedom of expression of "our" ethnonational being. Whatever the rival ethnonational group undertakes will be perceived as one more of "their" attempts to directly or indirectly jeopardize "our" people, reduce "our" rights, thwart "our" development, put "us" in an even more subordinate position. During ethnic times there are new, numerous, and by no means unimportant sources of dissatisfaction, anger, and the desire to "return in kind," in addition to the more or less ordinary sources of dissatisfaction and accompanying aggressiveness that are a part of daily life. This greatly increases people's aggressive potential, making them more inclined to act and react aggressively.

Belittling the other—the "rival"—ethnonational group is at the heart of every ethnonationalistic movement, every ethnonationalistic ideology. In 1995, David Archard fittingly noted that a nation is a community that is united by a common misconception regarding its origin, and a common antipathy towards its neighbors. Overrating the characteristics of people of your own ethnic group and underestimating people from a "rival" ethnonational group is the driving force behind the entire ethnonationalistic discourse and view of the world. This is why a pledge of tolerance, friendly relations, and successful cooperation among ethnic groups provides a fairly good balance between how one sees one's own ethnic group and how one looks upon other ethnic groups. During ethnic times, this ideal position is drastically upset: people glorify without exception their own ethnonational community, its past, its achievements, the characteristics and traits of its (ethno)national features, absolutely everything—from national cuisine to national literature. The religion, culture, past, and so-called ethnonational traits of the rival ethnonational group are judged quite negatively, of course. In short, there is not and cannot be anything positive about members of the "rival" ethnonational collective. "Nationalism," writes Isaiah Berlin, "is a belief in the unique mission of a nation, as being intrinsically superior to the goals or attributes of whatever is outside it; so that if there is a conflict between my nation and other men, I am obliged to fight for my nation no matter at what cost to other men; and if the others resist, that is no more than one would expect from beings brought up in a inferior culture, educated by, or born of, inferior persons, who cannot *ex hypothesi* understand the ideals that animate my nation and me" (1990: 177).

Viewed objectively, the differences between clashing ethnonationalist groups are characteristically neither large nor important. Most often the situation is quite the opposite: the differences are chiefly small and not enough to stand in the way of friendly relations and good cooperation between the groups. Small differences cannot in themselves be a justification or reason for hostility, and are even less so for efforts to destroy the members of another ethnonational group and expel them completely from some territory, which is what people carried away by ethnonationalistic passions quite often do. Small differences must therefore be transformed into big differences, which is exactly what ethnonationalists do,with the help of hatred.

Hatred blinds and destroys critical thinking. A man who is overcome by hatred sees and hears only what justifies his hatred, what gives it new momentum, and confirms the accuracy of its aim. When a man is angry at someone, he continually finds new excuses for his aggressive feelings: in that person's behavior, in his movements, intentions, his earlier proceedings, his real or presupposed plans. Hatred, just like aggressiveness, feeds on itself. Viewed objectively, small differences between two people or between two peoples are transformed by hatred into enormous, insurmountable differences. Hatred does not grow out of differences, it creates them. We do not hate those who are similar to us but those who are different from us.

What we have, though, is not just differences, but differences *per se*. As Michael Ignatieff notes, differences *as differences* are not so important: "no human difference matters much until it becomes a privilege, until it becomes the basis for oppression" (1998: 50). And that is exactly what happens with differences between ethnonational groups, differences that are the product of ethnonationalistic discourse, the ethnonationalistic need for differences. Differences between "our" ethnonational group and the "rival" group are such, the ethnonationalists reason, that they not only exclude any form of living together but greatly justify "our" efforts to move the members of the other ethnonational group as far away as possible, to eliminate them in various ways, or force them to accept "our" culture, religion, customs. The subtext is quite clear. "Our" culture, "our" view of the world, "our" habits and inclinations are superior, more valuable, worthy of being preserved and spread. This cannot be said of the "rival" ethnonational group, its culture, its members' habits and customs.

Finally, we should not forget one other important source of the rise in both aggressiveness and aggression in ethnonational times. When the ethnonationalists' behavior, manner of thinking, and feeling become the social standard, people's aggressiveness and aggression are turned not only towards the "rival" ethnonational group but also towards members of their own ethnonational collective, who, for any reason whatsoever, are different from the social norm or even openly oppose it. Everything that actually or potentially sets the individual apart from his ethnonational collective is the target of ethnonationalists' aggressiveness and aggression, and must be eliminated as soon as possible.

In brief, during ethnic times people become aggressive who are not by nature inclined to aggressiveness, and those who have been prone to violence of any kind become even more aggressive and inconsiderate. Ivo Andric summarized this unique time in the following description:

> People were divided into the tormented and the tormentors. The hungry animal living in man that dares not appear until the obstacles of good behavior and laws have been removed had now been liberated. As often happens in man's history, violence and looting, and even killing were tacitly allowed, under the condition that they were in the name of higher interests, under circumscribed slogans, against a limited number of people, with a specific name and specific convictions. A man with a clear conscience and open eyes living at that time could see such a spectacle as an entire society was transformed in a day (1997: 282–83).

WORKS CITED

Andric, I. *The bridge on the Drina*. Translated by L.F. Edwards. Chicago: University of Chicago Press (1st ed. 1945), 1997.

Archard, D. "Myths, lies, and historical truth: A defence of nationalism." *Political studies* 43 (1995): 472–81.

Berlin, I. *The crooked timber of humanity*. Princeton, NJ: Princeton University Press, 1990.

Ignatieff, M. *The warrior's honor: Ethnic war and modern consciousness*. London: Chato and Windus, 1998.

Kakar, S. *The colors of violence*. Chicago, London: University of Chicago Press, 1996.

Ethnic Stereotypes in the Writings of Croatian and Serbian Psychiatrists

Psychiatrists' participation in the most recent conflicts in the Balkans can be viewed from several angles. They can be viewed by psychiatrists (1) as national leaders, such as, Radovan Karadzic, formerly leader of the Serbian Democratic Party (SDS) in Bosnia; Jovan Raskovic, founder of the SDS in Bosnia; (2) as prominent members of leading political parties, such as, Slavica Djukic-Dejanovic, formerly deputy president of the Serbian Social Party (SPS); Aleksandar Taskovic, a prominent member of the Serbian Radical Party (SRS); (3) as being not ready, in a multicultural environment at a time of growing ethnonationalism, to indicate their patients' mounting tendency to turn for help to psychiatrists with whom they share the same ethnic origin, and so on.

The writings of Croatian and Serbian psychiatrists that analyze the ethnic features of the Croats and the Serbs are an interesting and revealing aspect of psychiatrists' participation in the ethnonationalism-inspired conflict between these two ethnic groups. Moreover, the authors of these writings are among the most distinguished representatives of their profession, and the writings appeared in the period from 1991 to 1999.

Psychiatrists do not analyze and describe ethnopsychological features very often; that is more the job of social psychologists and anthropologists. Psychiatrists appear here and there as members of research teams whose task is to identify and study the national character of an ethnonational group and possibly find an explanation in historical, political, economic, and other circumstances for what are ostensibly socially conspicuous traits in the national character of a specific ethnic group, or simply traits that those initiating and financing such research consider particularly interesting and important.

It is true, however, that during ethnonationalistic times psychiatrists have been known to accept the job of analyzing the national characteristics of rival or opposing groups. In Richard Brickner's "The German Cultural Paranoid Trend" (1942), he finds paranoid traits in the German people's national character (megalomania, suspicion, feelings of persecution, a tendency to use the projection mechanism, the consciousness of having a special mission, etc.). And in Kenneth Appel's 1945 paper "Nationalism and Sovereignty: a Psychiatric View," he first establishes the existence of certain parallels between the opinions of individuals and entire peoples that lead to warfare, as well as the fateful consequences for both the individuals and peoples caused by isolationism, and traditional, tribal ideas of sovereignty.

During conflicts among groups, interest focuses primarily on the enemy's national character, but there is also interest in the character of one's own ethnonational group. To put it succinctly, an answer or partial answer is sought in the national character of the enemy—i.e., rival ethnonational group— to the questions: Why did the conflict arise? Why does the enemy behave as it does?

On the other hand, quite as expected, conflict and warfare have a great impact on the development of antagonistic views among conflicting groups, with the inevitable attribution of exclusively or mainly bad traits in the national character of our enemy, along with an embellished image of ourselves. Previously neutral opinions by the members of one group about the other are turned into negative opinions, and manifest or latent negative opinions become even more negative. For example, the Americans' opinions about the Germans and Japanese became considerably more negative during and immediately after the Second World War. Stereotypical opinions that the Indians had about the Chinese underwent the same fate in 1959 when relations between these two countries deteriorated. Gertjan Dijking, writing about national identity and geopolitical visions, notes that on few subjects do ideas rely so much on quotations and on echoing the opinions of others as does national character (1996:88).

Ethnocentrism and ethnonationalism played an important role in fomenting war in the former Yugoslavia, particularly conflicts between the Croats and the Serbs. These conflicts were inevitably reflected in the image the Serbs and Croats had about each other. The writings of Croatian and Serbian psychiatrists published between 1990 and 1999 that are devoted entirely or partially to describing the ethnic character of the Serbs or Croats greatly confirm the accuracy of this last statement.

In order to better understand the writings under discussion in this chapter, it would be helpful to view them within the broader context of ethnocentrism, ethnic stereotypes, and national character.

ETHNOCENTRISM, ETHNIC STEREOTYPES AND NATIONAL CHARACTER

At the very beginning of this century, William Graham Sumner defined ethnocentrism as "this view of things in which one's own group is the center of everything, and all others scaled and rated with reference to it."

> Every group nourishes its own pride and vanity, boasts itself superior, exalts its own divinities, and looks with contempt on outsiders. Each group thinks its own folkways the only right ones, and if it observes that other groups have other folkways, these excite its scorn ... The most important fact is that ethnocentrism leads a people to exaggerate and intensify everything in their own folkways which is peculiar and which differentiates them from others. It therefore strengthens the folkways (Sumner 1906: 12–13).

In the broader sense, ethnocentrism implies people's strong attachment to their ethnic group, with the symbols or values of other groups becoming the object of scorn and hatred. Nationalism, when it comes on the historical scene, not only advocates that a people is constituted as a political community, and "that it is the nation which is the ultimate object of political allegiance, and that one's fundamental political identity derives from membership of the nation" (Poole 1999: 32); it also implies that the nationalist's own nation should be dominant among other nations, and that a good number of characteristics of our conationals are more praiseworthy than the respective characteristics of members of other national group(s). Ethnonationalism, as a collectivistic-authoritarian form of nationalism, by its reification (and deification) of (ethno)national community, does it to an even greater extent.

Thus, it is not difficult to see that ethnocentrism and ethnonationalism share some common features such as an uncritical preference for one's own group and underestimation of other groups, with attendant ethnic stereotypes.

Numerous theories have tried to explain the origin and dynamics of ethnocentrism and ethnonationalism. The most important are: the sociobiological theory, the theory of the authoritarian personality, the theory of frustration and aggression, the theory of group solidarity, and the theory of social identity.

Since I will discuss ethnic stereotypes later in the text, I will turn my attention here to a syndrome that is essential to ethnocentrism, *amity inside, enmity outside*, and will briefly elucidate it from the social-psychological viewpoint.

The group mentality or need to belong, either innate or acquired, is one of the most powerful driving forces in man. It spurs man to numerous activities whose true meaning can only be deciphered with the help of the group mentality as some sort of heuristic principle. In other words, within the specific features of group mentality lie the answers to many questions that arise when a man starts to think about ethnocentrism and its meaning for the individual and the group.

When considering the role that group mentality plays in the development and expression of ethnocentric views and convictions, it should not be forgotten that man is a social animal not so much because he fraternizes with all people without discrimination but because he likes in particular to fraternize with a specific group of people. It is therefore unfounded to believe that men's propensity to destroy one another, which is partially based on the belief that members of other (ethnonational) groups belong to another species, can be done away with if people start to believe that they all belong to one large group—mankind. That loyalty to a group, which is much smaller than mankind, is one of the essential characteristics of human beings, makes it extremely hard to transform the biological fact that all people belong to one species into a political and psychological reality. With only slight exaggeration, it might be said that it is inhuman to expect people to psychologically identify with mankind. They practically never do. And should the interests of mankind and their own group ever come into conflict, it is not hard to predict which side will win. After all, real psychology is always (or should be) in tune with psychological reality.

What is the relationship between the feeling of belonging to the group, basic group identity, and ethnic (i.e., national) feelings? In the era of nationalism our group identity is closely connected with (ethno)national identity. Today, Julia Kristeva notes, a foreigner, an outsider, is primarily defined in terms of his or her nationality. In the world of nation-states "the foreigner is the one who does not belong to the state in which we are, the one who does not have the same nationality" (1991: 96).

The development and maintenance of group cohesion, in the concrete case of an ethnic or national group, should not be neglected when discussing the nature of ethnocentrism. Group cohesion unquestionably develops and intensifies by insisting on the exceptional qualities of members of one's own group, on their duty to obey group norms, be loyal to the group, and actively participate in carrying out its goals.

Drawing support from Freud's dictum in his book "Totem and Taboo," Kristeva maintains that excluding "others binds the identity of a clan, a sect, a party, or a nation," and at the same time is "the source of pleasure of identification ('this is what we are, therefore this is what *I* am') and of barbaric persecution ('that is foreign to me, therefore I throw it out, hunt it down, or massacre it')" (1993: 50).

Within the context of analyzing the social-psychological basis of ethnocentrism, the key question is: Does growing group cohesion necessarily result in negative, even hostile, views towards those who are outside "my" group, thus members of other groups? The answer is yes. Every increase in intergroup cohesion, practically without exception, antagonizes those who are not members of "my" group.

Since the existence of another group—regardless of whether it is a real or only a potential source of danger for "our" group—increases group cohesion, it is often hard to say what is the cause and what is the effect, whether increased

group cohesion causes hostile feelings towards those outside
the group, or whether the hostility of those outside the group
brings about group cohesion.

I said that the pattern of *amity inside*, *enmity outside* is at
the very heart of the ethnocentric view of the world. This pattern, however, is not only characteristic of ethnocentrism; it is
a common component of the psychology of all large groups.
Ethnocentrism relies on this characteristic of group psychology and abundantly exploits it.

Ethnic stereotypes are the unfounded, unproven views
and convictions of one ethnonational group about other
ethnonational groups or their representatives. Ethnic stereotypes have the same characteristics and serve the same pur-
pose as other stereotypes. They are usually group related and
refer to one or more groups. In other words, there are no individual stereotypes. Stereotypes use shortcuts, so to speak, in
the thinking process. They assume that hackneyed judgments about someone or something are objective conclusions
confirmed by analysis. Stereotypes are always part of a
group's broader views, understandings and convictions, and,
as a rule, maintain the group's views and beliefs. Furthermore, stereotypes are always judgmental, evaluative. They
are never neutral.

In order to understand the relationship between ethnocentrism as a whole—particularly its basic characteristics of
aggrandizing the members of one's own group and belittling
the members of another or other groups—and ethnic stereotypes, we can use the concept of "prejudice" as a sort of inter-
mediary concept. Prejudice is an attitude towards a specific
object (individual, group, etc.) that is not based on experience
with the object of the prejudice and is therefore difficult to
change. A negative ethnic attitude can be considered prejudice because there is a great similarity (overlapping) between ethnic prejudice and ethnic stereotype. It is broadly
accepted that an individual with ethnic prejudice uses ethnic

stereotypes to rationalize the hostile feelings he fosters towards a particular ethnic group or groups.

Of course, this is not the sole function of stereotypes. According to the structuralist-functionalist concept, stereotypes define the nature of different social groups, either within broader society or outside it. In this way stereotypes support norms of behavior expected from the group and individual and suggests how they should be treated. From the conflict viewpoint, stereotypes justify or rationalize existing patterns of inter-group relations. Finally, on the social level, stereotypes have a valuation-expression function. By expressing stereotypical convictions, the individual confirms that he is part of the system of convictions he represents, which assures membership in the group. Ethnic stereotypes carry out to a great degree all three of these functions of the stereotype.

Based on what has been said about ethnic stereotypes and their relationship to ethnocentrism, it is clear that ethnic stereotypes are a manifestation of ethnocentrism on the level of views and convictions. There are no ethnic stereotypes without ethnocentrism. What is the link between national (ethnic) character and ethnocentrism or ethnic prejudice? They are interdependent to the extent that ethnic (national) stereotypes mean imputing certain characteristics, specific traits of national character, to a certain people or ethnic community.

The very concept of national character is problematic, burdened by many dilemmas. Does national character exist at all? Is national character the same thing as modal personality (as used by Ralph Linton, 1945), or is it the same as the basic structure of personality (as used by Abraham Kardiner, 1939)? Does national character correspond to those personality characteristics most often encountered in a society, or those that are most desirable for that society (which would correspond to Fromm's (1947) concept of social character)? Does national character include relatively long-lasting personality characteristics (preferential defense mechanisms, how one acts towards oneself and others, the concept of self, etc.) or phenotypes of changing behavioral patterns and convictions? Can national character be noted and identified only between people of the same nationality or same ethnic origin who live together in the same (geographical, cultural, historical, social, political) circumstances, or is it relatively easy to note among all people of the same nationality (same ethnic origin) regardless of the social-cultural circumstances in which they live and the influences they are/have been exposed to? Do all members of the same nation or ethnic group have the same national character, or does it vary depending on the social-geographical region, social-economic class, and so on? Is national character a sharply delineated entity, or do different peoples and ethnic groups have a large number of the same personality characteristics so that it is very difficult, if at all possible, to single out one or more characteristics distinctive of the national character of a specific people? Is there a correlation between the distinctive personality patterns that can be established using research methods such as questionnaires, projection techniques, interviews, analyses of collective behavior, institutional practices, rituals, systems of belief, and the image of national character held by group members, on the one hand, and members of other national-ethnic groups, on the other? Finally, what image of one's own or others' national character has a greater influence on how people act towards those from the same or other ethnic groups: the image of national character that results from lengthy, impartial research or the image that has been formed by political events and interests, as well as historical, political, economic, and other relations between said peoples or states?

It is hard to believe that any significant change in the image of one's own or other people's national character will come about by scientifically founded indicators. As a rule, political and economic events and interests cause such changes. Changes in the British notion of the French and German national character that took place within only a few decades illustrate this last statement.

Until 1904 most of the English had regarded the French with suspicion, and self-righteous disdain, as immoral, flighty, and frivolous. France had been their enemy through the centuries; and as for its morals—well, look at Paris! The English had also considered Germans almost as honest, serious, home-loving as themselves. This was what they were taught. Suddenly, they were told to reverse their opinions. The French, they learned, were a noble folk, sadly misunderstood. Look how fond King Edward was of the Parisians, and they of him. As for the Germans, they were trying to steal Britain's trade, they aimed at building a navy to rival the British; they were a danger and must be very carefully watched. Almost overnight the English obediently took up these new attitudes—hostility to Germans, friendliness with the French. The ten years' preparation for war began on both sides. (Fyfe 1940: 33–34)

Today, as integration processes in Europe are gaining momentum and Britain is preparing to take a serious and broader role in them, the German national character is very likely not being presented anywhere nearly as negatively in the eyes of the English as was the case during both world wars.

It seems hard not to agree with Steve Reicher et al. (1997) that the idea of national character is theoretically and empirically inadequate. First of all, it serves the specific ideology of nationalism, and, viewed more broadly, it is an attempt to explain complex cultural, ideological, and structural forms by reducing them to notions of individual psychology.

ALLEGED ETHNONATIONAL CHARACTERISTICS OF THE SERBS AND CROATS

According to Klein (1992), professor of psychiatry at Zagreb (Croatia) University, the Serbs are "known for their militant tradition"; they cherish "the cult of warriors and military leaders." The group cohesion of the Serbs is formed around warrior-leaders. The Serbs often have an inferiority complex in relation to the Croats and the Slovenes, the ethnonational groups in the western part of the former Yugoslavia, "because they are aware of their lower level of civilization and culture." They "try to get rid of these feelings (of inferiority) by means of various defence mechanisms, such as negation, projections, denial, ambivalence, but in any case a destructive component is very often present." The Croats, however, Klein states, have built their own cohesiveness on labor, dialogue, obedience, and the expectation of understanding and justice.

Jakovljevic (1992), professor of psychiatry at Zagreb University, argues that the Croats and the Serbs differ primarily in regard to their respective political cultures. The Serbs, in his account, have a paranoic political culture, the main features of which are "megalomania, expansiveness, hegemony, and pathological possessiveness." The characteristics are "the reflection of a grandiose self, and represent, in fact, a pathological defense against a deeper sense of inferiority." Another feature of the Serbian paranoic political culture, according to Jakovljevic, is destructiveness. The latter is "related to a nihilistic self ('black hole'), with the destruction of others resulting eventually in self-destruction." In contrast, he maintains that the Croats are the protagonists of a political culture of peaceful coexistence. They are a freedom-loving, civilized nation with a thousand-year-old culture and tradition.

What is the origin of these differences in their political cultures? The Serbian cultural tradition belongs to Byzantine (Orthodox) civilization. One of the major characteristics of the "Serbian Orthodox religion is that it is a part of the national identity rather than a religious symbol integrating into Christian civilization." Besides, "militant tradition is a significant part of Serbian collective identity and self," and the Serbs have "an almost erotic attitude towards weapons." As for the Croats, their political culture belongs to Western civilization and the European tradition of the Roman Catholic Church. Jakovljevic, like Klein, states that the tradition of the Croats is based on faith, work, obedience, dialog, and justice.

Maric (1998), professor of psychiatry at Belgrade (Serbia) University, has a completely different view than his Croatian colleagues about the national-cultural characteristics of both his own people and the Croats. He states that the Serbs have always been well intentioned towards other peoples: they are not militant. In a paper dealing with the effects of economic sanctions on health, Kalicanin (1994), who is also a professor of psychiatry at Belgrade University, agrees: "We, the Serbs, take pride in the fact that we have never resorted to bad-mouthing or vilifying other peoples" (1994: 11). Maric proceeds to point out that the Serbs are Orthodox in terms of religion, and that "Orthodox religion is not militant. Unlike other religions, the Orthodox religion respects the religious affinities and preferences of peoples. In contrast, the Islamic and Catholic religions are very militant; their followers want to expand and impose their views on other peoples" (1998:72). In addition, Maric claims, the Serbs are a clever, resourceful people (1998:134); they are rich in spirituality (1998: 20); and, they have an intense spiritual life (1998: 17). Furthermore, he asserts, the Slavs have much more capacity for empathetic behavior than other peoples do. However, "people living in the countries of today's Western civilization [and Croatia is supposed to belong to that civilization] do not have enough time for other people. They are in good measure egoistical; not keen on giving themselves to other human beings. The Slavs, in general, and the Serbs in particular, can still do so" (1998: 56–60).

People in the West, Maric argues, exercise a nonauthentic kindness with the use of expressions like "Have a nice day" and "Have a nice weekend." They are accompanied with an obligatory smiling face and sometimes with one or two other courteous phrases. "And it is superficial, empty. It is completely different when you meet our [meaning the Serbian] people. They are ready to listen to you in an authentic [untrained] way; to show genuine interest in your problems; to tell you something intimate about what has been bothering them—in other words, they are ready to give themselves completely to you" (1998: 61).

The Serbs, Maric continues, have never reached a high standard in the production of material goods and objects.

> It is obvious that the accumulation of objects has not been of great interest to them. This indicates they are committed to the spiritual qualities of life. They have not been enslaved by objects like the people in the West [including the Croats, of course]. However, if the Serb does praise some object, he does so because of its spiritual meaning, rather than because of the money he gets for it . . . This confirms our thesis that spirituality is a general feature of the Serbs (1998: 180).

WHO DOES WHOM FRUSTRATE?

Jakovljevic states that the Serbs have been frustrated by a great many factors. The examples he cites are: the collective exaltation of the Croats that followed the elections in Croatia; the process of collective mourning for and valediction of the Croatian victims of the Communist regime; and, the rehabilitation of political victims and prisoners, many of whom have become the new Croatian leaders. All of these factors—together with the fear of the unknown and the arrival of democracy, the likelihood of losing unjustly obtained privileges, and, in some cases, the fear of responsibility for the abuse of power—"have markedly increased the frustration and anxiety of the paranoid political mind," that is, of the Serbs.

However, Maric asserts, it is the Serbs who have frustrated the Croats for years, and this is why the Croats have, for the most part, looked down on them. Why should the Croats feel frustrated by the Serbs? Because, according to Maric (1998:77), the Serbs have for so long witnessed the weakness, failures, wrong-doing, and defeats of the Croats.

When the Serbian Borderlands (Krajine) were set up in the fifteenth century, the Serbs came to protect the Austro-Hungarian monarchy (and the Croats) from the Turks. In other words, the Croats were far too weak to protect their (Austro-Hungarian) state. Furthermore, in the First World War, the Serbs, who were on the side of the victors in the war against Austria-Hungary, virtually freed the Croats from their centuries-old enslavement; they accepted them as brothers in the Kingdom of the Serbs, Croats and Slovenes, later called Yugoslavia. In the Second World War, it was as if history repeated itself for the third time. The Croats, who had formed the so-called Independent State of Croatia, a puppet regime of the Nazis, again experienced a dramatic defeat as an ally of Hitler. Once again the Serbs saved them and forgave their mistakes (1998: 78).

Given the above, Maric argues, it is small wonder that the Croats feel largely frustrated by the witnesses of their inferiority, the Serbs.

Paranoid Peoples and Victims

It is interesting that both the Croatian and Serbian psychiatrists largely use psychoanalytical vocabulary and schemes in explaining the respective structures of the personality of the Croats and Serbs and in identifying the underlying causes of their alleged deep antagonism and almost unavoidable conflict.

Gruden (1992), professor of psychiatry at Zagreb University, states that "in the Serbs, regressiveness prevails over progressive psychic tendencies." When the Serbian group regresses, he claims, the regression reverts to the level of the schizoparanoid position, while in the case of the Croats, the group regression is closer to the depressive position. The Serbs cannot integrate the self (i.e., the good and bad parts of the self).

> At first, such a regressive unintegrated and scared (disunion of the personality causes great fear) person projects the bad parts of his self and his previously introjected objects towards the outside. This is practically manifested in accusing others, and transferring to them all his negative characteristics . . . The present projections of the Serbian negative emotions onto the Croats have a *paranoid character* (italics by V.G.).

Conversely, Gruden states, "the capacity for sublimation is an important trait of the Croatian nation." Sublimation is a very demanding psychic mechanism; it requires effort. If the environment provides the support and the appropriate conditions for sublimation, sublimation is more likely to be pursued. "Persons of Serbian nationality have no group support in terms of sublimation." Quite the reverse, "the support provided by their group, legalizes a more regressive behavioral pattern. In contact with the other group (the Croats) which has much more successfully mastered the capacity for sublimation, a person of Serbian nationality feels guilt and envy." In comparing themselves with Croats, the Serbs become aware that "sublimation at a considerably higher level than their own is possible." And how do they react to such a perception? Confined to the "frames of a deeply regressive group," the Serbs cannot help attacking the source of frustration. "Hence the source of destruction and the impulse to demolish everything that is related to the Croats."

Raskovic (1990), the late professor of psychiatry at Belgrade University, had a very different view of the major source of Serbian-Croatian conflict, and of who is the aggressor and who is the victim. He asserts that the Serbs have "all the features of the Oedipal character" (1990:128). This means that "the Serbs are, to some degree, simultaneously aggressive and submissive. They are loyal and obedient, but, at times, prone to rebelling and to standing up fiercely against authority" (1990: 128). The Oedipal character is very open-minded. There are not many shades to it; in many situations it acts according to the principle of all or nothing. However, the Croats have the features of the castration character.

> This character is closed and inwards-orientated. Actually, most of the time, such a personality is distraught with the fear of being castrated; of something terrible that is going to happen to him/her, and of losing something that belongs to him/her. This personality type is afraid of being deceived, of being fooled by someone, and of being subjected to some unpleasant treatment that will endanger his/her dignity (1990: 130).

According to Raskovic, one may describe the Serbian-Croatian conflict as "the conflict between two ethnic groups, one of which is oedipal, somewhat aggressive and prone to initiate changes, while the other's members have the traits of the castration character—they prefer the status quo and are afraid of any change whatsoever" (1990: 130). In other words, "one ethnic group is always ready to change; its members are ready to change their fathers, their masters, and those who have appropriated pleasure; the other group is afraid of any change because it might bring about castration."

Basically, "people who have a castration type of personality structure are obsessed by a fear of those who have aggressive oedipal traits. They display enormous hatred towards *Oedip*, think there is nothing wrong with destroying aggressive *Oedips*, and do not think they should feel guilty if they kill them" (1990: 131). Hence, the conclusion that the Serbs cannot help being the victims of the Croats.

Jakovljevic has the opposite view of who is the victim in the Serbian-Croatian conflict. He contends that the Croats are not only victims of the Serbs, but also "of their own narcissistic benevolence and naiveté." Because the Croatian culture of peaceful coexistence has some features of a narcissistic political culture, the Croats narcissistically identify with the great democracies in the world, in order "to reduce the fear of unarmed Croatian people of the potential aggressor (the Serbs) which later proved justified." Jakovljevic does not want to be mistaken. He reminds us that there are two kinds of narcissism: healthy and pathological. He contends that "after the elections, Croatian political culture had tended to achieve the goals of healthy narcissism, such as the development of democracy and a peaceful/nonviolent political culture."

CONCLUDING REMARKS

Croatian and Serbian psychiatrists' writings about the national character of the Croats and Serbs have shown a typical *ethnocentric position:* they presented biased positive views towards members of their own ethnic group and biased negative views towards other groups. In a word, the schismatic in-group/out-group differentiation that van der Dennen (1987) speaks of is obvious in the writings of Croatian and Serbian psychiatrists.

The authors of these papers do not mention the possibility that the national character traits of their group or the opposing ethnonational group are unevenly distributed among all members of these communities. In other words, according to them all the Serbs are the same and all the Croats are the same. Van Dijk accurately noted that this dimension of ethnic prejudice is "sometimes seen at its most racist core, because it is along this dimension that in-group members feel superior to out-group members and, hence, entitled to the priorities, privileges, and power that underlie the other prejudice categories" (1987: 210).

Having a stereotypical view of someone means expecting that person to have certain characteristics by virtue of belonging to a certain group. Stereotypes, particularly ethnic stereotypes, can also have other functions. They help people defend or preserve their own value system, and they contribute to the creation and maintenance of group ideologies that justify various social actions. During ethnonationalistic times, these functions of ethnic stereotypes become socially much more important than in peaceful times, hence, people who produce and spread ethnic prejudices are in greater demand. When ethnonationalism has captivated people's hearts and minds, few people are prepared to raise their voice against prejudices that elevate "ours" and degrade "theirs."

Finally, the ethnic stereotypes of Croatian and Serbian psychiatrists might be explained by their need not to differ from but rather to conform to the spirit of the day. It has been well noted that conformism is the key concept in understanding differences in the degree of prejudice in groups and in individuals.

WORKS CITED

Appel, K. "Nationalism and sovereignty: A psychiatric view." *Journal of Abnormal and Social Psychology* 40 (1945): 355–363.

Brickner, R. "The German cultural paranoid trend." *American Journal of Orthopsychiatry* 12 (1942): 611–632.

Dijking, G. *Identity and geopolitical visions.* London, New York: Routledge, 1996.

Fyfe, H. *The illusion of national character.* London: Watts and Co., 1940.

Gruden, V. "Psychological sources of the Serbian aggression against the Croats." *Croatian Medical Journal* 33 (1992): 6–9.

Jakovljevic, M. "Psychiatric perspectives of the war against Croatia." *Croatian Medical Journal* 33 (1992): 10–17.

Kalicanin, P. "Nasilje nad zdravljem (Health as a victim)," in P. Kalicanin et al. (eds.), *Stresovi rata (The stresses of war)*. Belgrade: Institute for Mental Health, 1994.

Kardiner, A. *The individual and his society: The psychodynamics of primitive social organization*. New York: Columbia University Press, 1939.

Klein, E. "Yugoslavia as a group." *Croatian Medical Journal* 33 (1992): 3–13.

Kristeva, J. *Strangers to ourselves*. Hemel Hempstead: Harvester/Wheatsheaf, 1991.

Kristeva, J. *Nations without nationalism*. New York: Columbia University Press, 1993.

Linton, R. *The cultural background of personality*. New York, London: D. Appleton-Century, 1945.

Maric, J. *Kakvi smo mi Srbi (What we are like, the Serbs)*. Belgrade: Published by the author, 1998.

Poole, R. *Nation and identity*. London, New York: Routledge, 1999.

Raskovic, J. *Luda zemlja (Crazy country)*. Belgrade: Aquarius, 1990.

Reicher, S.; Hopkins, N.; and Condor, S. "The lost nation of psychology," in C.C. Barfoot (ed.), *Beyond Pug's tour. National and ethnic stereotyping in theory and literary practice*. Amsterdam, Atlanta, GA: Rodopi, 1997.

Sumner, W.G. *Folkways*. New York: Ginn, 1906.

Van der Dennen, J.M.G. "Ethnocentrism and in-group/out-group differentiation: Review and interpretation of the literature," in V. Reynolds et al. (eds.), *The sociobiology of ethnocentrism: Evolutionary dimensions of xenophobia, discrimination, racism and nationalism*. London, Sydney: Croom Helm, 1987.

Van Dijk, T.A. *Communicating racism: Ethnic prejudice in thought and talk*. Newbury Park, London; New Delhi: Sage, 1987.

Prove You're a Serb

A few days ago a middle-aged woman came into my office. She was quite upset, tense, and also highly distrustful. She spoke with a strong Zagreb dialect. She hesitated, looking inquisitively at the walls of my office where my medical diplomas are displayed. I had the impression that she wanted to be sure of something before she described her psychic discomfort. She asked me when I had come to Sydney, when and how my degree had been recognized, which part of Yugoslavia I was from and how long I had lived there, and finally, what my first name was, since there was only an initial next to my surname on the door of my psychiatric office and in the telephone book. Then she looked at me fixedly and after a long pause asked the question that I think she had wanted to ask the moment she entered my office, a question so crucial that the fate of our relationship depended on my answer. She asked me what my nationality was.

I answered—not quite sure whether she made a clear distinction between ethnic and national affiliation—that in the ethnic sense I was a Serb and that I was a Yugoslav in terms of my political-emotional affiliation; in other words, I joked that I was a citizen of a country (nation-state) that had disintegrated almost a decade ago. I could see that she was only partially satisfied with my answer. Her inquisitive look turned sharp and even piercing, as though there was something more she was anxious to find out that would definitively establish me as either an acceptable or unacceptable psychiatrist for her. She finally asked me how I could prove I was a Serb. I was taken aback by this question. No one had ever asked me to prove I was a Serb. I tried to think of a way to satisfy her request, but without success. I told her clearly and concisely that I had no proof I was a Serb. Inwardly I was agitated by this question. I wanted to react more pointedly. Why had she asked me that question? By what right? In daily life, and particularly in my professional life, I have been raised and trained not to make distinctions between people based on their ethnic affiliation.

On the other hand, I guarded against reacting strongly to the request to prove I was a Serb. I knew quite well what had happened and was still happening in most parts of former Yugoslavia. Members of all ethnonational groups had done a great deal of wrong to those who were not from their same group. Thus, I had to respect my prospective patient's need for her therapist to be of the same ethnic origin. I had to understand and have consideration for something I never would have tolerated in peaceful, not to say "normal," times. I, as a professional, could not and dared not allow my patients' ethnic origin to influence my opinion of them, or allow ethnic origin to influence my choice of patients, regardless of what I have lived through, how much I have suffered at the hands of those who justified their aggression against me by the simple fact that I am a Serb. In my capacity as a psychiatrist, I will have to understand the need of people from the Balkans to find a psychiatrist who shares their ethnic affiliation.

Clearly dissatisfied that I was not able to present any proof that I was a Serb, the woman kindly took leave of me, saying she would give me a call if she decided she wanted me to treat her. I never saw her again.

Ethnic affiliation was a key category in the recent war of "everyone against everyone" in almost the whole territory of the second Yugoslavia, and it continues to be as a determining factor in the relations in each of the states created after the disintegration of the Yugoslav state. The more I thought about it, the question asked by this woman not meant to be my patient seemed less and less absurd. If, in the recent (and only recent?) history of the Balkans, ethnic origin proved to be such an important, fateful dimension that determined (and in many places still determines) whether someone would get a job or be fired, whether someone would live or lose his or her life, whether someone would hold onto her personal property or have it taken away, whether someone would continue to live where he or she always had or been forced to flee without looking back, then, logically speaking, the ethnic affiliation of every person would have to be quite clear, incontestable, easy to notice and even easier to prove. Just looking at a person, or exchanging two or three words with him/her, would have to make it crystal clear—if we're speaking of the Balkans—that before you are a Croat, Muslim, Serb or a member of some other ethnic community. Ethnic affiliation had to be as clear and unmistakable as national affiliation, particularly since it has been shown that the former is far more important for the destiny of the individual and family than the latter. If someone is interested in your nationality, you show her/him confirmation of your citizenship or simply your passport, and all doubts and hesitations disappear. You need no additional proof, certificate, or confirmation.

In most countries, however, ethnic affiliation is not written into any personal document. Attempts to determine a person's ethnic affiliation by means of their first or last name often result in grave mistakes. There is no small number of first and last names that make it extremely difficult, if at all possible, to determine a person's ethnic origin. There are many examples. My father-in-law, a Serb, told me that in Sarajevo, which was primarily Muslim during and after the war, he had the habit of giving just his last name (Cecez) whenever he wanted to hide his ethnic identity. (Momir is a Serbian Christian name, and the family name Cecez is difficult to identify in ethnic terms.) On several occasions in the past 10–15 years, receptionists in Zagreb hotels openly or surreptitiously, but invariably in a friendly manner, let on that they knew my wife Dubravka was a Croat, although she isn't. On the other hand, in 1992 when she sought refuge in Belgrade during the Bosnian war, almost every time she was introduced to people there was a quiet comment that her first name was "a little" unusual. (Dubravka is a Christian name shared by both the Croats and the Serbs, although much more common among the Croats.)

Belonging to a specific religion might serve as a guidepost for identifying someone's ethnic affiliation, owing to the link between ethnicity and religion. But most often religion is not written in personal documents either. The way someone crosses herself/himself is hard to use as proof that someone is, say, a Catholic Croat or an Orthodox Serb. In addition, the number of people who have never been baptized is by no means small. Thus, it might happen that people, forced to cross themselves by someone who wants to determine their ethnic affiliation at any price, may make a mistake that is often fatal.

Furthermore, the language a person speaks and his/her accent are also unreliable guides in determining ethnic affiliation. Many Serbs who used to live in Sarajevo continue to speak like the Sarajevo Muslims and/or Sarajevo Croats for years after leaving that town. The speech of the Serbs in Zagreb is in no way different from that of the Zagreb Croats. In terms of a special culture being one of the essential determinants of an ethnic group, Serbs living in an environment where there are many Croats are very familiar with the myths and customs of the Croats, just as Croats who have lived in Belgrade for years are almost invariably well acquainted with the Serbs' customs, habits, patron saint (slava) feasts, culture.

People's ethnic identity is given to them; their hands are tied in this regard. They cannot change, or choose, except when their parents are of different ethnic origins. During times of crisis, such as civil wars, ethnic identity becomes a vital determinant. Isn't it strange, then, that for conditions in the Balkans and other areas such an extremely important characteristic, as unchangeable as gender or the color of one's eyes, is practically impossible to authenticate with clear, convincing, tangible proof. The fact that someone knows and feels that he or she belongs to a specific ethnic community and its cultural matrix, of course, is contained in his/her empirical, experienced, subjective world. It cannot be seen. Belief does not have the strength of proof.

Nonetheless it has been shown time and again that those who kill, maim, and exterminate people of another ethnic origin, systematically or in a campaign, practically never err in their choice of victim. They don't need proof of someone's ethnic affiliation. Why? Because either they were already acquainted with their future victims or else someone pointed them out, someone who had known them for years, decades. Civil war must be preceded by long years of living with or in the close vicinity of ethnic community members. People's ethnic identity is only revealed when you have known someone for a long time. It is shown through rituals, spiritual creations, and familiarity with certain myths and mythical personalities.

But first and foremost it is expressed in people's actions and reactions during times when ethnic identity becomes important and, more than important, unavoidable. During ethnic times everyone acts ethnically. Otherwise, when meeting someone for the first or second time, his/her ethnic identity passes unnoticed, particularly when someone, as happened

to me, is unable to present any proof of his/her ethnic origin.
When we met, my not-meant-to-be patient, and I must have
been living in different times: she in ethnic times, and I in
non-ethnic times.

Reactive Ethnonationalists

I have heard people from the Balkans lament more than once that "we" never would have rooted so strongly for "our side" (meaning members of their own ethnonational group), defended only "our" interests so passionately and fanatically, and been almost blinded to the rights and needs of "those others" if "we" hadn't seen how "those others" just care about their own business without regard to what might bother "our side," what might jeopardize, trouble, hurt, or humiliate "us." In other words, "those others" are to blame for the fact that "we" have become the same as "they" are—ethnonationally biased, rooting for "our side," inclined to aggrandize the defects of "those others" and read bad intentions into almost everything "they" do and say; at the same time "we" are quite prepared to find excuses for the obviously evil actions of "our side" and public deportment that is not the least peace-loving. In other words, people from the Balkans reason that "those others" are to blame for what "we" are. "They" have turned us into persons "we" never were before. (And in a slightly confessional manner, they add that they are not very happy with the way they are.) However, their current behavior and views were the only possible answer to "those others" extolling and pushing only "their" side, belittling and jeopardizing "our" side, trying to encroach on what is "ours."

What is the meaning of these explanations of ethnonationalist views and feelings that usually come from people who feel a little uncomfortable in the role of ethnonationalists? Where does this need to justify themselves come from, their poorly hidden desire to relieve themselves of the greater part of the responsibility for their ethnonationalistic digressions? What are the indications of joining the company of ethnonationalists in this manner?

Assuming that we go along with the above-cited motives for ethnonationalistic bias, or blindness, such a generation of ethnonationalism points to its reactive nature. I am not the one who decides whether I will accept and propagandize ethnonationalistic views. My decision to be an ethnonationalist is not the result of my free choice; it is not the consequence of having considered different possible forms of relations with people from my own ethnic group and "those others," analyzing the best, most useful form of relations for one or both sides. I have been reduced to a passive, inactive being, to Pavlov's dog who reacts this way or that depending on what is offered, on what external stimulation is applied at a given moment. "Those others" set my behavior. I only have the illusion that I decided of my own accord to be an ethnonationalist, that I did it to parry "their" ethnonationalism, to respond to it in kind, out of need, spite, or self-protection.

In essence, I had very little to do with adopting ethnonationalistic views and convictions. I became an ethnonationalist because "those others" acted like ethnonationalists. If "those others" had acted differently towards "our side," my view of the world would be as far from being ethnonationalistic as it was before they offered necessary and sufficient reason for my ethnonationalism. "Those others" are the ones who decide whether and how much of an ethnonationalist I become, not I. "They" have closed the door to the broad range of possibilities that were in front of me; "they" have reduced them to a single bad possibility.

The collective, group mentality is another important aspect of opting for ethnonationalism in this manner. If I submit to the ethnonationalistic treatment of "our side" and "those others" because I claim that "those others" were the first to scorn and persecute "our side" just because we are not part of their ethnic group, then I see "them" as a more or less uniform group. "Those others" are a group subject. "They" are one. I see no individuals in the mass of "those others." If I hadn't forgotten—or wanted to forget, which turns out to be the same thing—that "their" ethnonational group consists of individuals, I would have had to accept that it is more than likely that all of "those others" do not share the same views and feelings. I, however, prefer to take a cognitive shortcut and repeat that "they" are all the same. All the Serbs are Chetniks; all the Croats are Ustashe; all Bosnian Muslims are fanatical advocates of a "holy war." Thus, my view of "those others" is reduced to the collective "they." If and when I communicate with one of "them," I am actually communicating with "him/her" as a representative, an image, of the collective he or she belongs to. I am unable to see the individual—with all his/her doubts, fears, suspicions, proclivities—for the collective.

I use the same process of individual depersonalization with my own ethnic group whenever I explain, or rather justify, my own ethnonationalistic convictions and feelings by the ethnonationalism of the members of other ethnonational groups. I then take away my right to react as an individual. I am completely identical to my ethnonational group. Regardless of my individual experience with the members of other ethnonational groups, the very fact that "those others" act antagonistically towards "our side" is reason enough for me to act the same way towards "them." At that moment I actually abandon everything that comprises my individuality. I renounce the right to be unique and unrepeatable, which is the pride of every man, and I agree to be like all the others on "our side." I do not exist outside of "our side." My reaction is determined by my being a member of a specific collective and not by my own convictions, views, principles, feelings of justice. When the voice of the collective drowns out the voice of the individual within a person, he or she loses spontaneity, as well as the ability to create new views or new relationships, the impetus for which cannot be found in external influences.

In this sense the ethnonationalist who seeks justification for what she/he is by the fact that "those others" are the way "they" are, is showing that he or she has forsaken individuality and spontaneity. The actions and reactions of a spontaneous person are always more or less unexpected. He or she rarely falls into the trap set by those who count on uniformity in people's actions and feelings in certain circumstances. Reactive ethnonationalists rarely surprise anyone. Their reactions have been accurately foreseen by those who have played the card of ethnonationalism to succeed in their intentions. Reactive ethnonationalists are their safest bet, their most solid support. Were they not certain that a large number of people would start to think, feel, and act like ethnonationalists simply because "those other" ethnonationalists think, feel, and act that way, the planners of ethnonationalistic ideologies and movements would never muster the courage to use ethnonationalism as a means to achieve the goals that are so important to them.

I wonder if there is a way to make reactive ethnonationalists understand how fettered, lacking in spontaneity, and depersonalized they are when, sometimes hesitatingly and sometimes self-confidently in order to hide their internal discomfort, they claim they are ethnonationalists only because others made them that way.

Obsession with Ethnicity

During the summer of 2000, I was in Sarajevo again after several years and gave a lecture entitled "The Other Guy Is Always the Nationalist" at the forum of Bosniak Intellectuals. (Several years previously, the Bosnian Muslims officially changed their name to the Bosniaks.)

The Serbs and Croats I met who heard that I was to speak at this forum were surprised. They believed that I, as a Serb, had no place there. There would be almost exclusively Bosniaks and intellectuals from Arab countries and, they said, ideas and views were often heard that had little in common with the three most numerous peoples in Bosnia living together peacefully. Some of these Serbs and Croats reproached me, both openly and in private, for my planned lecture. They said that this forum—one of the most important, if not *the* most important in town—had been used on several occasions to rekindle anti-Croat and anti-Serb feelings. There were also those who saw my planned public lecture as currying favor with the Sarajevo Bosniak establishment.

And they did not hesitate to say it to my face. My disbelief regarding the accuracy of their remarks about the forum and my response that it was much more important what someone said than where he said it were not met with understanding.

The lecture itself was very well attended. The first two rows were filled primarily with older people who, it seemed to me, regularly attended more or less all the lectures, regardless of the topic. There were quite a lot of young people in the auditorium behind them. The lecture was followed by a discussion. They asked me why Serbian nationalism was genocidal. They asked for a detailed description of the characteristics of Serbian nationalism. Then they asked me to tell president Milosevic that the Bosniaks are a good and peace-loving people, which certainly could not be said of the Serbs. In response to my remark that the Kosovo myth is one of the favorite themes of Serbian ethnonationalism, a man in the audience who said he was a history teacher went into a lengthy explanation. He said that everything that is written and said about the Battle of Kosovo which, as everyone knows, is one of the key events in the history of the Serbian people, did not correspond to what actually happened on the Kosovo battlefield. All the questions indicated without fail that the people in the audience, or at least those who asked questions, saw me as someone from the "other side," someone who could not be part of "us." In order to remove any possible confusion about where I belong, one of the questioners started out by stating, or rather recalling, that I was born in Belgrade and am a Serb.

I lived in Sarajevo for almost half a century and never felt I was not a component part of that environment. My best friends in Sarajevo were—and, I would add, still are—people who are not ethnic Serbs. This was not because I chose my friends among people who were not of my ethnic origin, but because at the time we happened to be in the same place: in the same classroom, in the same year at the university, in the same health care institution. I do not doubt that everyone in prewar Sarajevo knew that my family were Serbs, but in daily communications no one ever let on that they knew. I acted the same way in communications with people of the same or different ethnic origin as mine.

After the lecture and the reactions and comments that preceded and followed, it was clear to me that the time had passed when people's ethnic origin was disregarded (perhaps, in accordance with the definition of nation as politicized ethnicity, it would be better to say ethnonational origin); rather, the ethnic community a person belonged to was of great concern. It had become an unavoidable dimension, something almost like a reflex that automatically came to mind when addressing, or even just thinking and speaking of, another person. The constant awareness of who is of what ethnonational origin does not have to be accompanied by strong emotion. It is simply some sort of general guideline, indispensable knowledge about every person that precedes any other information about her/him.

Caught by surprise, with a rather bitter taste in my mouth, I asked myself if I had truly, through no fault of my own, become a stranger in the town of my childhood, youth, and maturity. Why did almost everyone, both Serbs and the others, directly and indirectly remind me of the fact that I am a Serb? I ended my lecture with a rhetorical question: Why had I titled my lecture "The Other Guy Is Always the Nationalist?" Then I answered: to help listeners avoid the trap that many very quickly and easily fall prey to, in which they think that everything the speaker has said is true or mostly true, but that his words do not refer to them because, when it comes right down to it, isn't the other guy always the nationalist? Not a single question asked, and there were many of them, gave any hint that the audience had understood the danger of the ethnonationalistic conviction that "those others" were always the nationalists. Perhaps they simply did not want to believe that "their side" might be ethnonationalistic, too.

My impression that Sarajevo people know perfectly well, and take into account, who is a Bosniak, who is a Croat, and who is a Serb—with all the possible ways of using such knowledge for a broad range of purposes—was confirmed in the meetings I had with people during the several days I spent in town. It seemed to me that my very presence, or the fact that I am a Serb, induced most of the people I met to include one or more aspects of inter-ethnic relations in the conversation. At the same time, what they had to say made it quite clear that they saw me as a man with a specific ethnic affiliation.

So the Bosniaks found a way to remind me that the Serbs, in the milder version, had behaved out of proportion, and, in the stronger version, that the Serbs had behaved criminally towards their compatriots during the last war in the Balkans, especially in Bosnia. Should the conversation last for any length of time, I would hear that the Serbs were uncivilized, or rather that they were a people not inclined towards being civilized. That, ostensibly, was the essential trait of the Serbian people's ethnonational character. They had no doubts that every people has its ethnonational character, something that is innate and thus an unchangeable dimension. The Serbs, however, said, mostly in a lowered voice and a little conspiratorially, that they had suffered the most during the last war. They were twofold victims: of their compatriots firing from the hills around Sarajevo, and of the Muslims' lust for revenge. They talked about how difficult it is to be an ethnonational minority in the Balkans. They did not talk about how many Serbs took part in the great Evil. Either they passed over that in silence or found justification for it in the evil intentions and behavior of "those others."

Many of my collocutors switched very, very quickly from "you" to "yours" or to "we." It was clear that they did not see, or did not want to see, the individual behind the collective; to them the individual was only important as part of a larger group, in this case an ethnonational group. I was primarily interesting as a member of a collective and not as a man with specific interests, knowledge, inclinations, personal characteristics. My presence was simply associated with the Serbs, much, I believe, as the presence of a Bosniak would be associated with the Bosniaks, and a Croat with the Croats. I wondered whether I had once long ago, or in more recent times, made some statement, some remark, or had behaved in such a way that would explain such a reduction of my individuality to the collective I belong to. I need not emphasize how offended I was at being reduced to my ethnic group, at this abstraction that put my individuality between brackets.

Ethnic identity was the key dimension in the war in the second (former) Yugoslavia in the first half of the 1990s. Years after the end of the war people's ethnic identity had lost none of its meaning. People no longer die for it, but they continue to live for it. No small number of people live off it.

I have briefly presented my experiences of several days in Sarajevo because prewar Sarajevo meant a lot to me, and comparisons of the "Sarajevo of yesterday and today" are intrusive and hard to resist. It should be noted, however, that I found this same obsession with ethnicity in both Belgrade and Zagreb, where I spent several days before and after my stay in Sarajevo.

Looking back at how the Great Powers ended the war in the Balkans, Urs Altermatt, in the book *Ethnonationalism in Europe: Sarajevo Lighthouse* (1996: 11), notes that geopolitical peace was bought at the price of ethnic divisions. If these all-encompassing and powerful ethnic divisions—not just ethnoterritorial but divisions in the form of the above-mentioned generally widespread and obligatory preliminary knowledge about people's ethnic (ethnonational) affiliation—are the price that was paid for geopolitical peace in the Balkans, then this obsession with ethnicity, with its concomitant need for ethnic distinctions, is praiseworthy and welcome. After all, didn't someone say long ago that peace has no price? Or maybe it does: an exorbitant one.

WORKS CITED

Altermatt, U. *Das Fanal von Sarajevo: Ethnonationalismus in Europe*. Zürich: Verlag Neue Zürcher Zeitung, 1996.

For Further Reading

Adorno, T.W.; Frenkel-Brunswik, E.; Levinson, D.J.; and Sanford, R.N. *The authoritarian personality*. New York: Norton, 1950.

Allport, G. W. *Personality: A psychological interpretation*. New York: Holt, 1946.

Alter, P. *Nationalism*. London: E. Arnold, 1989.

Altermatt, U. *Das Fanal von Sarajevo: Ethnonationalismus in Europe*. Zürich: Verlag Neue Zürcher Zeitung, 1996.

Anderson, B. *Imagined communities: Reflections on the origins and spread of nationalism*. London: Verso, 1991.

Andric, I. *The bridge on the Drina*. Translated by L.F. Edwards. Chicago: University of Chicago Press (1st ed. 1945), 1997.

Appel, K. "Nationalism and sovereignty: A psychiatric view." *Journal of Abnormal and Social Psychology* 40 (1945): 355–363.

Archard, D. "Myths, lies, and historical truth: A defence of nationalism." *Political studies* 43 (1995): 472–81.

Banton, M. *Racial and ethnic competition*. Cambridge: Cambridge University Press, 1983.

Barth, F., ed. *Ethnic groups and boundaries*. Boston: Little, Brown, 1969.

Berke, J.L. *The tyranny of malice*. London: Simon and Schuster, 1989.

Berlin, I. *The crooked timber of humanity*. Princeton, NJ: Princeton University Press, 1990.

Billig, M. *Banal nationalism*. London: Sage, 1995.

Brass, P. *Ethnicity and nationalism*. London: Sage, 1991.

Braunthal, J. *The paradox of nationalism*. London: St. Botolph, 1946.

Breuilly, J. *Nationalism and the state*. Manchester: Manchester University Press, 1982.

Brickner, R. "The German cultural paranoid trend." *American Journal of Orthopsychiatry* 12 (1942): 611–632.

Calhoun, C. *Nationalism*. Buckingham: Open University Press, 1997.

Carr, E. *Nationalism and after*. London: Macmillan, 1945.

Connor, W. *Ethnonationalism: The quest for understanding*. Princeton, NJ: Princeton University Press, 1994.

Deutsch, K.W. *Nationalism as Social Communication: An inquiry into the foundation of nationality*. Cambridge, MA: MIT Press, 1953.

Dijking, G. *Identity and geopolitical visions*. London, New York: Routledge, 1996.

Doob, L.W. *Patriotism and nationalism: The psychological foundations*. New Haven, CT: Yale University Press, 1964.

Duckitt, J. *The social psychology of prejudice*. New York: Praeger, 1992.

Enzensberger, H.M. *Civil wars. From L.A. to Bosnia*. New York: The New Press, 1994.

Eriksen, T.H. *Ethnicity and nationalism: Anthropological perspectives*. London: Pluto Press, 1993.

Francis, E.K. *Interethnic relations*. New York: Elsevier, 1976.

Fromm, E. *Man for himself*. New York: Rinehart, 1947.

Fyfe, H. *The illusion of national character*. London: Watts and Co., 1940.

Gellner, E. *Nation and Nationalism*. Oxford: Basic Blackwell, 1983.

Gillis, J. R., ed. *Commemorations: The politics of national identity*. Princeton, NJ: Princeton University Press, 1994.

Ginsberg, M. *Nationalism: A reappraisal*. Cambridge: Leeds University Press, 1963.

Glazer, N. and Moynihan, D., ed. *Ethnicity: Theory and experience*. Cambridge MA: Harvard University Press, 1975.

Greenfeld, L. *Nationalism: Five roads to modernity*. Cambridge, MA: Harvard University Press, 1992.

Greenstein, F.I. *Personality and politics*. New York: Norton, 1975.

Grodzins, M. *The loyal and the disloyal: Social boundaries of patriotism and treason*. Chicago: University of Chicago Press, 1956.

Gruden, V. "Psychological sources of the Serbian aggression against the Croats." *Croatian Medical Journal* 33 (1992): 6–9.

Halliday, F. *Rethinking international relations*. London: Macmillan, 1994.

Halpern, J. M. and Kideckel, D.A., ed. *Neighbors at war: Anthropological perspectives on Yugoslav ethnicity, culture and history*. University Park, PA: Pennsylvania State University Press, 2000.

Hastings, A. *The construction of nationhood: Ethnicity, religion and nationalism*. Cambridge: Cambridge University Press, 1997.

Hayes, C. *The historical evolution of modern nationalism.* New York: Russel and Russel, 1968.

Hertz, F. *Nationalism in history and politics: A study of the psychology of national sentiment and character.* London: Routledge and Kegan Paul, 1944.

Hobsbawm, E. *Nations and nationalism since 1780.* Cambridge: Cambridge University Press, 1990.

Hockenos, P. *Free to hate.* New York: Routledge, 1994.

Hutchinson, J. *Modern nationalism.* London: Fontana, 1994.

Ignatieff, M. *Blood and belonging: Journey into the new nationalism.* London: Vintage, 1994.

Ignatieff, M. *The warrior's honor: Ethnic war and modern consciousness.* London: Chato and Windus, 1998.

Isaacs, H.R. *Idols of the tribe: Group identity and political change.* New York: Harper and Row, 1975.

Jakovljevic, M. "Psychiatric perspectives of the war against Croatia." *Croatian Medical Journal* 33 (1992): 10–17.

Jervis, R. *Perception and misperception in international politics.* Princeton, NJ: Princeton University Press, 1976.

Jones, S. *The archeology of ethnicity: Constructing identities in the past and the present.* London, New York: Routledge, 1997.

Jurgensmeyer, M. *The new cold war: Religious nationalism confronts the secular state.* Berkeley: University of California Press, 1993.

Kakar, S. *The colors of violence.* Chicago, London: University of Chicago Press, 1996.

Kalicanin, P. "Nasilje nad zdravljem (Health as a victim)," in P. Kalicanin et al. (eds.), *Stresovi rata (The stresses of war).* Belgrade: Institute for Mental Health, 1994.

Kardiner, A. *The individual and his society: The psychodynamics of primitive social organization.* New York: Columbia University Press, 1939.

Kecmanovic, D. *The mass psychology of ethnonationalism.* New York, London: Plenum, 1996.

Kedourie, E. *Nationalism.* London: Hutchinson University Press, 1960.

Kellas, J.F. *The politics of ethnicity and nationalism.* New York: St. Martin's, 1998.

Kemilainen, A. *Nationalism: Problems concerning the work, concept and classification.* Yvaskua: Kunstantajat, 1964.

Klein, E. "Yugoslavia as a group." *Croatian Medical Journal* 33 (1992): 3–13.

Kohn, J. *The idea of nationalism: A study of its origin and background.* New York: Macmillan, 1944.

Kristeva, J. *Strangers to ourselves.* Hemel Hempstead: Harvester/Wheatsheaf, 1991.

Kristeva, J. *Nations without nationalism.* New York: Columbia University Press, 1993.

LeVine, R.A. and Campbell, D.T. *Ethnocentrism.* New York: Wiley, 1972.

Linton, R. *The cultural background of personality.* New York, London: D. Appleton-Century, 1945.

Llobera, J.R. *The god of modernity: The development of nationalism in western Europe.* Oxford: Berg, 1994.

Maric, J. *Kakvi smo mi Srbi (What we are like, the Serbs).* Belgrade: Published by the author, 1998.

Mayall, J. *Nationalism and international society.* Cambridge: Cambridge University Press, 1990.

McNeil, W.H. *Polyethnicity and national unity in world history.* Toronto: University of Toronto Press, 1986.

Minogue, K.R. *Nationalism.* Baltimore: Penguin, 1970.

Morgenthau, H.J. *Politics among nations.* New York: Knopf, 1948.

Mosse, G.L. *Masses and man: Nationalist and fascist perceptions of reality.* Detroit: Wayne State University Press, 1987.

Moynihan, D.P. *Pandaemonium*. New York: Oxford University Press, 1993.

Orwell, G. "Notes on nationalism," in S. Orwell and S. Angus (eds.), *Collected essays: Journalism and letters of George Orwell*, vol. 3. New York: Harcourt Brace Jovanovich, 1945.

Periwal, S., ed. *Notions of nationalism*. Budapest: Central European University, 1955.

Pfaff, W. *The wrath of nationalism: Civilization and the furies of nationalism*. New York: Simon and Schuster, 1993.

Poole, R. *Nation and identity*. London, New York: Routledge, 1999.

Raskovic, J. *Luda zemlja (Crazy country)*. Belgrade: Aquarius, 1990.

Reicher, S.; Hopkins, N.; and Condor, S. "The lost nation of psychology," in C.C. Barfoot (ed.), *Beyond Pug's tour. National and ethnic stereotyping in theory and literary practice*. Amsterdam, Atlanta, GA: Rodopi, 1997.

Rothschild, J. *Ethnopolitics. A conceptual framework*. New York: Columbia University Press, 1981.

Royce, A.P. *Ethnic identity. Strategies of diversity*. Bloomington: Indiana University Press, 1982.

Scheff, T. J. *The bloody revenge: Emotions, nationalism, and war*. Boulder, CO: Westview Press, 1994.

Schöpflin, G. *Nations, identity, power*. London: Hurst and Co., 2000.

Shafer, B.C. *Nationalism: Myth and reality*. New York: Harcourt, Brace and Co., 1955.

Smith, A.D. *The ethnic origins of nations*. Oxford: Basil Blackwell, 1986.

Smith, D.S. *Nationalism and modernity*. London, New York: Routledge, 1998.

Snyder, M. *Private appearances/Private realities*. New York: Freeman, 1987.

Staub, E. *The roots of evil: The origins of genocide and other group violence*. Cambridge: Cambridge University Press, 1990.

Stavenhagen, R. *The ethnic question: Conflicts, development and human rights*. Tokyo: University Press, 1990.

Stein, H. *Developmental time, cultural space*. Norman: University of Oklahoma Press, 1987.

Sugar, P., ed. *Ethnic diversity and conflict in eastern Europe*. Santa Barbara, CA: ABC-Clio, 1980.

Sumner, W.G. *Folkways*. New York: Ginn, 1906.

Symmons-Symonolewicz, K. *Modern nationalism: Toward a consensus in theory*. New York: The Polish Institute of Arts and Sciences in America, 1968.

Tamir, Y. *Liberal nationalism*. Princeton, NJ: Princeton University Press, 1993.

Van den Berghe, P. *The ethnic phenomenon*. New York: Elsevier, 1981.

Van der Dennen, J.M.G. 1987. "Ethnocentrism and in-group/out-group differentiation: Review and interpretation of the literature." In V. Reynolds, et al. (eds.), *The sociobiology of ethnocentrism: Evolutionary dimensions of xenophobia, discrimination, racism and nationalism*. London, Sydney: Croom Helm, 1987.

Van Dijk, T.A. *Communicating racism: Ethnic prejudice in thought and talk*. Newbury Park, London; New Delhi: Sage, 1987.

Index

Adorno, Theodor, 72, 73–75
Adriatic coast, 27
Aggressiveness, 33, 40, 47,
    50; of authoritarian per-
    sonality, 72; of
    ethnonationalists,
    129–30; of oedipal per-
    sonality, 152
Albanian, 33
Allport, Gordon, 118–19
Altermatt, Urs, 171
Amity inside-enmity out-
    side pattern, 141–43. *See
    also* Brotherhood in-
    side-animosity outside
Appel, Kenneth, 138
Archard, David, 132
Authoritarian personality,
    72–75

Balkans, 20, 161, 163,
    170–71
Bamburac, Jovan, 31
Baska Voda, 27
Belgrade, 24, 30–35, 61, 100
Belgrade University, 148
Berlin, Isaiah, 133
Blidinjsko Lake, 26–27
Blood and *soil*, 128
Bloodshed, 55
Bosnian Academy of Sci-
    ences and Art, 27, 31
Bosnian army, 98
Bosnian Croats: attitudes
    towards the Serbs,
    26–30; relations between
    the Bosnian Muslims,
    Bosnian Serbs and,
    88–93

Bosnian Muslims: advocates of holy war in ethnonationalist discourse, 165; attitudes towards the Serbs in war-torn Sarajevo, 22–24, 97–99, 168–69; ethnonationalist sentiments and, 168–71; irregular police forces of, 96; leadership of, 97, 102; management of town affairs during war time in Sarajevo; relations between the Bosnian Croats, Bosnian Serbs and, 88–93; Serbian Civic Forum and, 96–97
Bosnian Serbs, bombing of Sarajevo, 25; attitude towards their co-ethnics they suspect of not siding with them, 25; relations between the Bosnian Muslims, Bosnian Croats and, 88–93
Brickner, Richard, 138
Brotherhood inside-animosity outside, 114. *See also* Amity inside-enmity outside
Budapest, 33
Byzantine civilization, 147

Chetniks, 28, 165

Civil war, 99, 103, 161
Conformism, 71, 75
Conventionalism, 73
Croatian Academy of Sciences and Art, 27, 31

Dichotomization, 73
Dijking, Gertjan, 139
Djikic, Osman, 23
Djukic-Dejanovic, Slavica, 137
Domobrani, 61

Endemic ethnonationalism, 68, 71, 124
Enzensberger, Hans Magnus, 69
Epidemic ethnonationalism, 68, 71, 108, 124
Ethnic affiliation, 14, 20, 49, 106–8, 158–61
Ethnic anomaly, 107, 110
Ethnic cleansing, 49
Ethnic crossbreeds, 110–11
Ethnic prejudice, 49–50; definition of, 143; children from ethnically mixed marriages as a blow to, 111
Ethnic stereotypes, ethnonationalism, national character and, 139–46; propensity of authoritarian personality towards, 72–73

Ethnically mixed marriages, 121–22; children from, 105–11
Ethnocentrism, 69; definition of, 140; psychiatrists as mongers of, 137–54; sociobiological explanation of, 115, 117
Ethnonational identity, 23, 26, 30–31, 63; biological foundation of, 114; distinction between ethnic and national, 106–7; is given to people, 161; group identity and, 142; need for, 78; political identity and, 140; religion as a part of, 147; vital importance of, 171
Ethnonationalism, 140, 154, 164–65, 171; conflict inspired by, 137, 139; endemic and epidemic, 68, 87–94, 124; the individual and collective in, 65–75; inverse, 95–104; Serbian, 168
Ethnonationalistic mentality, 116
Extremism, 70

Faith, 17–20
Forum of Bosniak Intellectuals, 167
Fromm, Erich, 73, 144. *See also* Social character

Frustration, 47–48
Functional autonomy of motives, 118
Fyfe, Hamilton, 146

Gruden, Vladimir, 150

HDZ (Hrvatska Demokratska Zajednica), Croatian Democratic Community, 65
Herzeg-Bosnia, 26–28, 30
High self-monitors, 71
Holy war, 165
Home guard. *See* Domobrani

Identification: with the collective, 41; with one's own ethnic (national) group as guarantee of security and pleasure, 20, 142. *See also* Ethnonational identity
Ignatieff, Michael, 134
Inclusive fitness, 115
Independent State of Croatia, 61, 150
Interethnic marriages. *See* Ethnically mixed marriages
Internal emigration, 108
Intolerance, 120–30; as element of we-they syndrome, 70; ethno-

nationalism gives rise to,
129
Inverse ethnonationalism,
95–104

Jagomir Psychiatric Hospital, 35
Jakovljevic, Miro, 147–53

Kakar, Sudhir, 130
Kalicanin, Predrag, 148
Karadzic, Radovan, 25, 34,
96, 137
Kardiner, Abraham, 144
Kingdom of the Serbs,
Croats and Slovenes, 150
Kiseljak, 26
Kecmanovic, Dusan, 28, 30
Klein, Eduard, 146–48
Knin Krajina, 63
Kosovo, battle of, 168
Kristeva, Julia, 142
Kruna (Croatian money),
99

Language of blood, 48
Linton, Ralph, 144
Loyalty, 98, 105–11, 142

Machiavellianism, 51
Maric, Jovan, 148–55
Media war, in interethnic
confrontations, 84–86
Mental disturbance, 9,
37–44, 123–28

Mental sanity (health), 42,
43, 37–44, 123–28
Mentally underdeveloped,
40
Milosevic, Slobodan, 29, 34,
100, 101, 168
Montenegro, 33
Moralism, 73

Narcissism, 153
*Narcissism of small differ-
ences*, 80
National character,
ethnocentrism, ethnic stereotypes and, 139–46; of
the Serbs and Croats,
146–53
Nepotistic behavior, 117
Nin (magazine), 100

Orthodox religion, 148
Orwell, George, 68
Oslobodjenje (newspaper),
26

Paranoid peoples, 150–51
Parochialism, 68–70
Pavelich, Ante, 61
Political has-beens, 10
Political parties, 20, 34, 137
Poole, Ross, 140
Posusje, 27–29
Psychiatric clinic: in Bel-
grade, 35; in Sarajevo, 21,
23, 25, 29; in Split, 30; in
Zagreb, 31

Psychiatric Congress of Yugoslavia, 35
Psychiatrists, 22, 30–31, 34–35; exculpation of war crime perpetrators, 128; mongers of ethnonational stereotypes, 137–54; witnesses of social-political change, 9
Psychopaths, 49

Quisling forces, 61

Raskovic, Jovan, 151–52
Reicher, Steve, 146
Religious rights, 20
Religiousness, rise in, 20
Role models, 46
Roman Catholic church, 148

Sarajevo, 22–24, 34; electronic media in, 83–86; interethnic relations in pre-war, 88–94; Muslim dominated government in, 98
Sarajevo University, 59
SDS (Srpska demokratska stranka[Serbian Democratic Party]), 96, 137
Serbian Boderlands (Krajine), 150
Serbian Civic Forum, 96, 104
Serbian-Croatian conflict, 151–52

Serbian Orthodox religion, 147
Serbian paranoic political culture, 147
Slavs, 148
Smith, Anthony, 70
Social character, 73, 144. See also Fromm, Erich
Sociobiology, 114–15
Split, 26, 30
SPS (Socijalisticka partija Srbije [Serbian Social Party]), 137
SRS (Srpska radikalna stranka [Serbian Radical Party]), 137
Stup, 26
Sumner, William, Graham, 130–40

Taskovic, Aleksandar, 137
Theories of ethnonationalism, 141
Tito, Josip Broz, 18
Transitional period, 18–20; lack of normative framework during, 45–46; rise in faith during, 18–20; typology of social-political behavior during, 10–14; violence during, 45–52

Uglesic, Borben, 31
Ustaches, 60, 165

Van den Berghe, Pierre, 115, 117, 119

Van der Dennen, Johan, 153
Van Dijk, Teun, 153
Victim, 25, 51, 53–57,
    99–100, 153, 170
Violence, 45–52, 129, 135
Vreme (magazine), 100

We-they syndrome, 69–70
World War II, 11, 72,139, 150

Xenophobia, 69

Yugoslav army, 61
Yugoslavia (second, former),
    9, 171; intense need for
    faith and belief in the last
    days of, 17, people's men-
    tal health in, 37–42; the
    Serbs and Croats in,
    140–53

Zagreb, 31–32, 63–64, 157
Zagreb University, 150

About the Author

DUSAN KECMANOVIC is formerly professor of psychiatry and political psychology at Sarajevo University. He has published extensively in the field of social psychiatry, social pathology, and the psychology of ethnonationalism. Among his earlier publications are *The Abuse of the Mentally Ill* and *The Mass Psychology of Ethnonationalism*. Professor Kecmanovic left the war-ridden Balkans in 1993, and he has lived in Sydney, Australia since.

Printed in the United States
152795LV00001B/12/P